Love's Mysteries

The Body, Grief, Precariousness and God

Rachel Mann

CANTERBURY
PRESS
Norwich

First published in 2020 by the Canterbury Press Norwich
Editorial office
3rd Floor, Invicta House
108–114 Golden Lane
London EC1Y 0TG, UK
www.canterburypress.co.uk

Canterbury Press is an imprint of Hymns Ancient & Modern Ltd
(a registered charity)

Hymns Ancient & Modern® is a registered trademark of
Hymns Ancient & Modern Ltd
13A Hellesdon Park Road, Norwich,
Norfolk NR6 5DR, UK

British Library Cataloguing in Publication data
A catalogue record for this book is available
from the British Library.

978 1 786 22281 7

Typeset by Regent Typesetting
Printed and bound by
CPI Group (UK) Ltd

Contents

Acknowledgements

As ever, a book like this would not be possible without the love, support and wisdom of many friends, family and colleagues. I continue to be grateful, more than I can say, for the patient love of my parents, siblings and nephews. Even when they are bewildered by both the nature and intensity of my written projects, they are there for me. They keep me honest and sane. Thank you also to the congregation of St Nick's, as well as colleagues, for being prepared to indulge my academic fierceness and creative impulses. I am grateful to colleagues in Manchester Diocese who invited me to be the keynote speaker at the National Social Responsibility Conference in 2018, as well as to Dr Susie Snyder who invited me to be the keynote speaker at a Leavers' Event at Cuddesdon College. At each event I road-tested some of these ideas in this book. My gratitude also extends to friends at Hymns Ancient and Modern who gave me an opportunity to speak at the *Church Times* Festival of Preaching where further ideas were tested. I should also be lost without the immense love of my sisters, the Risen Women, as well as the support of friends and colleagues at the Manchester Writing School, Manchester Met University, and on the Church of England's Faith and Order Commission. I am very much not the first to have explored the themes contained in this book. I offer a footnote on the work of countless others, from Shelly Rambo through to Karen O'Donnell and beyond.

Introduction

Perhaps there is someone out there who has not known grief. I suppose it depends on how it is defined. If, by grief, one means the loss of a loved one, then it may be possible to live for quite a period of time before one encounters grief's sharp, bewildering and confusing effects. I was 11 before I became fully conscious of grief in this sense. The death of a grandparent triggered a flurry of emotions and signalled a whole new set of relations with the world, both private and public, inner and outer. I had to relearn how I related to the world. However, grief – as a word which gestures towards both emotion, as well as relationships with others – should not be so readily limited. Grief, understood broadly as bodies encountering the facts of loss, limit and fragility, is a kind of theme of the world. When one is born one loses the womb. One is born into grief. That first cry we all make as a baby is a cry of grief. I'm not sure we ever recover from this first encounter with loss. Nor should we. Otherwise, we might never quite learn how to live.

In many ways, this is a book about grief. However, as I hope my opening paragraph indicates, it is not a book about grief in the psychological or therapeutic sense of 'how might I cope with this particular grief I am feeling or experiencing?' As a spiritual director and priest, I have a great deal of respect for the processes and complexities of grief. I understand the value of schema like Kübler-Ross's stages of grief, and – heavens – there have been times in my life when therapeutic strategies have helped me cope. However, this book aims to examine the ways grief operates in the theological and philosophical realm. Lest anyone panic at that sentence, what I mean is that I am convinced – like many before me – that grief and what it tells us about human bodies helps us understand more about God and ourselves.

The power of grief and what it gestures towards – our relationships, our fundamental precariousness and limitations as creatures of flesh and bone – has long been important to me. Indeed, this book is arguably part of a loose trilogy.[1] In the first book, *Dazzling Darkness*, I sought to speak theologically and spiritually into the personal and particular facts of my life.[2] It involved an attempt to be unsparingly honest about my experiences of transitioning from male to female, and of ill health, from an almost unrelentingly first-person perspective. As one of my closest friends astutely put it, it is a lonely book. In the second book of this loose trilogy, *Fierce Imaginings*, I sought to examine the theological threads that run through a family caught up in world-shaking events – in that case, a world war – and how family, culture and country weave in and out of those practices one typically calls 'religion', 'ritual' and 'theology'.[3] It considers the strange and often-troubling inter-

---

1 There is something deeply appealing about trilogies. The notion is seemingly hardwired into the fabric of European culture, perhaps ultimately traceable back to the conceptual potency of the Trinity. The 'three-yet-one' mesmerizes and tantalizes both Christian and post-Christian, as well as wider European imaginations. Indeed, it has never surprised me that Freud, no great friend of religion, discerned a tripartite structure for human being, and the 'rule of three' plays out endlessly in our cultural imaginaries. Cinematic and literary universes are populated with trilogies, and trilogies of trilogies. Even if you don't much like it, *Star Wars* presents the popular trilogy manqué, but there are others, including *Lord of the Rings* and *Back to the Future*. Fantasy, especially children's fantasy – which so often deals with the loss of childhood, magic and enchantment – is rich with trilogy: *His Dark Materials* and *The Hunger Games*, to name two. Serious literature is awash with trilogy: John Le Carré's *Karla*, Hilary Mantel's *Wolf Hall*, and Pat Barker's *Regeneration* sequences. Perhaps the fascination with trilogy can be traced back to the earliest culture – consider Aeschylus' *Oresteia*.

2 Rachel Mann, *Dazzling Darkness* (Glasgow: Wild Goose, 2012). A second edition is due to be published in 2020.

3 Rachel Mann, *Fierce Imaginings* (London: Darton, Longman & Todd, 2017).

sections between 'memory' and 'memorialization'. While it began to wrestle with some of the social, political and cultural implications of memorialization, ritual and God, it remained centred on family. One family. My family.

Love's Mysteries, in one sense, widens the theatre once again. It is about bodies and, crucially, bodies under pressure. It is about what happens to bodies – mine, yours, potentially anyone's – when living under conditions of trauma; when violence is committed, or bodies are placed in pain and distress or pressure or isolation. It is about grief in this wider sense. It is about what it means to be enfleshed and, thus, what it means to live with fragility and what is sometimes called 'precarity'.[4] There is a profound sense in which we cannot be bodies, subjects, humans, without the facts of precariousness. Fragility is simply inscribed into life, life lived both badly and well.

Crucially, *Love's Mysteries* attempts to keep attention on the theological and philosophical possibilities of bodies thrown into a precarious world. It is not so much about family or about me, or even individuals, but community. It is about bodies as fragile community realities, existing in relationship with each other. It is about the kind of community that is possible in a fragile, compromised world. It is about those bodies when we place them in the context of a God who enters such fragility and compromise in Jesus Christ. I return again and again to the theatre of the body as it is found in political, human and theological nexuses and fields. Wherever I range I aim to come back again and again to this disputed and wondrous site: the body. Quite often that body is mine, but not always.

Love's Mysteries, then, is a series of explorations into the modes of 'precariousness'. I'm not going to lie. For the casual reader, I suspect a book about the 'precarious' doesn't exactly feel like a 'come-and-get-me' sort of subject matter. However, as the events of 2020 have definitively reminded everyone, the

---

4 I understand that, for some, the term 'precarity' will be experienced as a kind of linguistic violence, perhaps because they are uncomfortable with Americanisms or neologisms. I try to use it sparingly, but such is its traction – in academic discourse, at least – that its use is unavoidable.

precarious is everywhere. It should matter to each and every one of us. Precariousness is the stuff of life. The impact of Covid-19 on human culture, politics and economics may not be clear for a long time yet, but the coronavirus pandemic surely reveals, even to the most determined optimist, that everything we take for granted can be thrown up in the air at any moment.

If this book suggests that precariousness is the very substance of life then it also makes a bold claim: when properly contextualized, precariousness is a crucial dimension of the good life too. Fragility is inscribed into it. Precarity can seem abstract and perhaps a little intimidating, but the precarious is the substance of the everyday. For while someone who lives in a country such as the UK – at least before the impact of coronavirus! – could end up believing and acting as if their life or culture or way of going on is not especially precarious (and indeed is less precarious than the life lived by the vast majority in this world), there is a certain amount of self-deception about that. To live has an openness to it, which, despite our dreams of safety and attempts at insurance, has risk inscribed into it.

Indeed, after reading Judith Butler's book *Precarious Life* a few years ago, I began to encounter precariousness everywhere.[5] Precarious bodies, precarious lives, even precarious ideas. However, given the seeming solidity, stability and immutability of institutions and personal lives (of many) in a nation like the UK, I feel the need to adopt a variety of strategies to treat with it. In the context in which I live, even with the destabilizations of Brexit, an emboldened Far Right and a febrile Left, as well as pandemics and climate change, the idea of 'precariousness' has a kind of gift for elusiveness. To offer a definition of it – one that is actually useful rather than tautological – feels forever just out of sight. Add in the notion of the Living God – utterly real and yet seemingly so often absent or problematized – and one can feel like one is reflecting on matters that have the complexity and delicacy of a spider's web.

So, this book aims to be, by turns, poetic, analytic, playful, forensic and discursive. If that sentence creates the impression

---

5 Judith Butler, *Precarious Life* (London: Verso, 2004).

that reading *Love's Mysteries* will induce dizziness, please do not be alarmed! I hope that the chapters in this book – which cover subjects ranging from the politics of grief through to the readiness with which our bodies give up on us and on to the glorious fragility of relationship – will be disruptive. However, there is another side: God is most alive in these places of precariousness and fragility. Jesus Christ is not afraid of embodiment. Christ knows our precariousness from the inside. This is thrilling and terrifying and indicates the extent to which Christ not only participates in the worlds we know, but invites us into the fullness of life, in all its fragile wonder and precarious love. In a time when we are negotiating the meaning and effects of a viral pandemic, I am minded of those words of Simone Weil written to a long-distant friend: 'Let us love this distance, which is thorough woven with friendship, since those who do not love each other are not separated.'[6] The fullness of life and friendship has glory and cost inscribed into it.

This book takes its title from a brace of lines written by John Donne: 'Love's mysteries in souls do grow,/ But yet the body is his book.' These lines are taken from his poem 'The Ecstasy', a substantial and profound meditation on the possibilities of love and desire between souls. Donne reflects on the extent to which love is a matter between souls – arguably immutable, timeless, eternal things – growing closer together either in platonic or divine love. At this level, it is beautiful and inspiring, giving the reader a sense of love as ultimately unsullied by the precarious facts of the body. However, Donne – never afraid of the demands of love and ecstasy in the lived realities of this world – ultimately notes that love is inscribed in bodies, those ever-changing, particular and mutable things. Or, if not quite that, that love is met in the intersection of soul and body. It is seen and unseen, revealed and elusive. The body is a sign of grace. However, there is a sting: if the body is a

---

6 Included in a letter to her friend, Gustave Thibon. For more information, see Maria Popova's website, 'Brain Pickings', at www.brainpickings.org/2015/08/24/simone-weil-friendship-separation/ (accessed 04.05.2020).

sign of grace, it is something which is inevitably marked by change, vicissitude and death. Grace is located in something which decays, is compromised and breaks.

Throughout this book I attempt never to lose sight of this commitment to the belief that the body is sacramental. For some people of faith such a commitment is likely to appear as offensive. It is, undoubtedly, the case that Christianity has often seemed to have a downer on the body. However, in the midst of some wide-ranging meditations on the possibilities of precariousness, I return again and again not only to the goodness of the body but its holiness. I suggest that part of its holiness lies in its capacity to show grief; indeed, to hold it in its very sinews. I'm not going to lie. Some of the examples I consider, including the catastrophe of the Manchester Arena bombing, rightly raise serious questions about the limits of grace, grief and forgiveness. Others, including chapters on the way pregnant bodies or disabled bodies have been represented, seek to remind the reader that not all bodies have been treated as equal.

The axis of celebration, promise and hope in this book is ultimately the body of Christ. This is a body which is simultaneously utterly ordinary – for how else could it hope to be representative? – as well as utterly strange in its holy possibilities. This is the body on which we are invited to feast and be fed. This is the body in which God's living community is invited both to participate and become part of. This is the body that is Love, in its utter precarity and its eternal possibility. When we live in and on this body – when we are conformed into its skin, bone, its subatomic encodings, its trauma and its transformations – we are pitched out of ourselves into glorious precariousness. We cease to seek after saving ourselves and abandon our strategies of control, and our need to ameliorate precariousness. We open ourselves to the world. We embrace our fragility. We become precarious for Christ and feel hope surge through the code, the flesh, the fractures of our own compromised bodies.

Who is Worthy of Grief?

On the evening of Monday 22 May 2017, I was doing what I often do on Monday evenings after a long day of meetings, ministry and conversation: I was sitting in front of my laptop scrolling through my Twitter timeline. It was just another Monday evening, full of the usual mix of carping, argument, comedy cats and cynical humour. Then something started to happen. Tweets began to emerge from people in Manchester city centre that indicated something very serious was happening. There was talk of loud noises, possibly even explosions, near the MEN, aka the Manchester Arena. As ever, with such immediate Twitter reportage, information was, initially, mixed and confusing. Something had happened, for sure. It might be a bomb, but it might equally be an accident. Quite quickly, images and short videos began to emerge, some from people who had been attending the Ariana Grande concert at the Arena, some from people in the nearby parts of the city centre. Images of the emergency services arriving in the Victoria Station area of town began to appear. Something dreadful had happened.

At 10.31 BST, a suicide bomber detonated an improvised explosive device in the foyer area of Manchester Arena. It contained nuts and bolts, which acted like shrapnel, flying in every direction. That evening over 14,000 people had attended the Ariana Grande concert at the venue. Many of them were children, for Grande was famous not only as a singer but as a children's entertainer on the Nickelodeon show *Victorious*. As the concert hall emptied, the foyer area was full of happy gig-goers and their parents. In the aftermath of the suicide bomber's act, nearly two dozen people were killed and scores were injured, many with physical and psychic wounds that might never fully heal.

The 2017 Manchester Arena bombing presents an intense focus for the varieties of grief. There are many other sites of trauma, of course, and I shall attempt to explore some of them. However, the Arena bombing, certainly for someone like me who lives in the city, remains exceptionally poignant. There are layers and horizons of grief within it that warrant cautious attention and I want to offer my reflections on it with care and tenderness. I do not want to mock or diminish anyone's sense of grief, including those who, it might seem to the casual observer, were on the margins of trauma. While the primary grievers were surely those who directly lost loved ones, there was a potent sense in which the grief generated by the Arena bombing was public, widely felt and interpersonal.

For, in this social media age, grief is partially constructed and structured in multi-platformed and transnational ways. For days, the centre of Manchester found its locus in the laying of flowers in St Ann's Square. Public, interpersonal grieving was negotiated through a sea of fragrance and colour. Layers upon layers of flowers acted as metonyms for layers of emotion, some simple, some no doubt sophisticated, all felt sincerely. For over a week after the bombing, the square felt like the hub of the world's media, full of cameras and satellite trucks gathered at the edges of the main square. This media was hungry for content. For that week, it was a risk to walk through the square while wearing a dog collar, for priests were seen as public figures with an angle to offer on grief and hope. I knew priest friends who, when they had to go into town, simply took their dog collars out.

Manchester city centre provides a focus for over 2 million people. Since its renaissance in the late 1990s, it has grown to provide a cornucopia of delights. It can – especially during rush hour – feel a busy and congested place. However, in the week following the bombing there was something else. It was almost possible to taste the emotion in the diesel of the buses that choke Oxford Road and John Dalton Street and Deansgate. The streets were swollen with bodies and grief and love. St Ann's Square – that august, almost severe square named after the late Stuart church at its south end – moved and flowed endlessly with hundreds, thousands of people who wanted to signal their respect, their shock, their grief. Most had no direct connection to the bodies they grieved over. Attention was fixed on the tokens of grief ever growing in the heart of the square. Though I know many drew comfort from going into the church, attention was drawn away from it towards the central bouquets of grief. Indeed, I recall attending an archdeacon's visitation at St Ann's that week (when the Cathedral was closed) and being stunned by the bright lights of the TV cameras intensively facing away from the church. St Ann's felt at the margins not only of the world's attention but of its own square.

When we talk about grief or grieving we enter space and time framed in terms of hardship, suffering and bodily affliction. To grieve can mean to make angry or enrage. It has horizons of lament. In Old French, it has implications of injustice, and misfortune and calamity. It also gestures towards burden and oppression. In its Latin root, to grieve means make heavy or weighty; to have weight. So, when we begin to ask, 'Who is worthy of grief?' we might also be asking, 'Who has weight?', or 'Who is weighty in our culture, our communities, our bodies and lives?' And, in a hint of how liturgy and poetics begin to emerge, who is worthy of memorialization and language and song? Who can be re-membered in discourses of pain and anger and injustice and oppression, as well as joy and hope?

In the aftermath of the Manchester bombing various narratives took hold. One of those narratives – a very impressive one – was the 'we shall not be divided by violence; we are united; we shall model peace'. Religious and political leaders, including my bishop in Manchester, provided a united front. There were moving moments when religious leaders came to the sites of grief and joined their silence to that of others. As I've indicated on numerous occasions, including directly to the Bishop of Manchester himself, I think David Walker was exceptional under intense pressure. He demonstrated the kind of nuanced carefulness and bold grace that the Church of England has, at times, failed to model. He understood that, though he was a significant community leader in Manchester, he was one among many. In one sense, as a diocesan bishop of the Established Church he had every right to stand in public places and demonstrate spiritual leadership. However, what was especially impressive was how he intuitively understood that the old days when the C of E spoke first as of right are gone. He entered the space of grief with the gentleness of a guest invited on to holy ground.

Another axis of attention concerned the sheer impact of the destruction. The juxtaposition between the work of violence and the fact that people were out for a night of fun only heightened the effects of the bombing. People had gone out for a good time, to listen to a winsome children's entertainer. The roll call of death was appalling. In one sense, the contrast between the vile act of terror and the context should make no difference. And yet, of course, it does. Sometimes the gap between the violence and the wider context is partially constitutive of the horror.[1] Either way, in a modern liberal democracy the death of 22 people in one incident is a lot. Although, of course, that's where a line is revealed. That night, 23 people died. One happened to be the bomber Salman Abedi.

On 29 May 2017, the local newspaper, the *Manchester Evening News*, wrote, 'It is important to remember the innocent victims and not the terrorist who murdered them.' Let us be clear, Abedi perpetrated an act of terror. I understand why one would want to say that he is not worthy of grief or remembrance. I understand why words would be withheld from the perpetrator of violence. Abedi's denial of the good – his action's *privatio boni* or absence of good – makes him unworthy of word, of sermon, of song, of poem. His work

---

1 These kinds of juxtapositions have been noted by writers caught up in catastrophic situations. In *Fierce Imaginings*, for example, I note how writers like Sassoon felt that the good weather on the First Day of the Somme only acted to seal the tragedy in memory. See Rachel Mann, *Fierce Imaginings* (London: Darton, Longman & Todd, 2017), pp. 51ff., for more.

of violence arguably denies him the worth, weight or value of liturgy or memory.

But it is noteworthy to think, from a Christian perspective, what it means for a body to be erased from the record. To be placed beyond the line of value. To have been so othered that a human is not even listed among the dead. It is a pungent, startling indication of the limits and lines that can be drawn through grief – through weight and value, and therefore of language. There are things that become unsayable, or at least profoundly risky about, for example, the extent to which Abedi himself was a victim of ideological exploitation or perceived injustices around identity and the West's violence. Perhaps I go too far and make a category mistake in this particular case, but even if I am wrong about Abedi, it is striking how cultural affinity, skin colour, notions of nationality matter in the theatre of grief.

And here's the fascinating thing. It's at least tempting to suggest that one of the ways communities and persons locate their sense of oneness, and disavowal of violence, and the path from grief to action (which of course includes revenge and fighting back as well as more pragmatic compromises and acts of love) is by processes of othering. There are invisible or barely tangible lines of value that when pressure comes can harden or become defined. I was struck by the complexity of reaction in my parish after the attack. I had conversations with people who were scared for their Muslim neighbours because Abedi might be seen as representative of all Muslims; and I met and spoke with people who did want to lash out at what they saw was a problem with Muslims or Arab men. Abedi was for them a metonym for Muslim savagery.

This example may raise more questions than answers and still seem to hover above our concerns in the Church perhaps. But I wonder if we are to be agents of grace we cannot become hardened to the limits of grief, because they signal some-thing about our (and the diverse wider communities') senses of justice, suffering, oppression and value. The limits of grief indicate where lines of community and memory are delineated. In *The Ethics of Memory*, the philosopher Avishai Margalit explores – in part through an analysis of the ethical afterlife of the Shoah – 'the healing power of knowing the truth in the case of communal memories'.[2] He notes, however, how 'memory breathes revenge as often as it breathes reconciliation'.[3] In so far as ethics is the province of community,[4] memory – who or what is remembered and considered valuable – intersects powerfully with grief. Grief is not and should not be reducible to an emotion or emotions 'experienced' by individuals, but is a horizon of community. Margalit speaks of 'thick relations'. These are anchored in a (perceived) shared past or 'moored in a shared memory'.[5] On this picture, 'memory is the cement that holds thick relations together'.[6]

In *Precarious Life*, the philosopher Judith Butler asks, 'Is there something to be gained from grieving, from tarrying with grief, from remaining exposed to its unbearability and not endeavouring to seek a resolution for grief through violence?'[7] She presents us with a challenge: to consider whether, in staying with the sense of loss, we are left feeling only passive and powerless, or whether we become alert 'to a sense of human vulnerability, to our collective responsibility for the physical lives of one another'.[8] Butler is not considering individual grief here – though, of course, individuals experience it – but grief as a mode of communal vulnerability. Writing in the shadow of 9/11 and the USA and Britain's decision to invade Afghanistan and Iraq, Butler wants to invite us to reflect on how grief – as vulnerability and openness to others who wound us and whom we may wound – may transform our human relations. As she summarizes:

---

2 Avishai Margalit, *The Ethics of Memory* (Cambridge, MA: Harvard University Press, 2002), p. 5.

3 Margalit, *The Ethics of Memory*, p. 5.

4 Whereas, for Margalit, morality is the work of individuals. See Margalit, *The Ethics of Memory*, p. 8.

5 Margalit, *The Ethics of Memory*, p. 7.

6 Margalit, *The Ethics of Memory*, p. 8.

7 Judith Butler, *Precarious Life: The Powers of Mourning and Violence* (London and New York: Verso, 2006 (2004)), p. 30.

8 Butler, *Precarious Life*, p. 30.

Could the experience of a dislocation of First World safety not condition the insight into the radically inequitable ways that corporeal vulnerability is distributed globally? To foreclose that vulnerability, to banish it, to make ourselves secure at the expense of every other human consideration is to eradicate one of the most important resources from which we must take our bearings and find our way.[9]

The violence generated in the shadow of 9/11 and the war in Afghanistan, of which the Manchester Arena bomb was arguably part, can invite us – as Butler suggests – to consider the attempts of wounded, grieving persons, governments, countries to foreclose their sense of vulnerability by revenge. The motive for this foreclosure is, unconsciously or consciously, to strike back at their perceived injustice and make themselves 'safe'. One of those strategies was, in the aftermath of 9/11, to use invasion for revenge and to make 'the West' safe. However, as I've begun to outline, I sense that tarrying with grief – while incredibly risky, for it may become a fixed point, from which there is no ready escape – may represent an unexpected resource when faced with making a response to fractured, divided communities and societies. Butler suggests:

To grieve, and to make grief itself into a resource for politics, is not to be resigned to inaction, but it may be understood as the slow process by which we develop a point of identification with suffering itself. The disorientation of grief – 'Who have I become?' or indeed, 'What is left of me? What is it in the Other that I have lost?' – posits the 'I' in the mode of unknowingness.[10]

Grief pushes us towards mystery; it disorientates and perhaps makes new meanings possible.

---

9 Butler, *Precarious Life*, p. 30.
10 Butler, *Precarious Life*, p. 30.

Judith Butler does not, as far as I'm aware, count herself as a person of faith. However, her political analysis of grief surely unexpectedly creates space for theological and religious reflection: in destabilizing ideas about the 'I' or the subject as self-reliant, isolated and invulnerable, she exposes what it means to be human to relationship and connection to the Other. She reminds us of our fundamental indwelling in each other. We are, as Christianity and the great faith traditions have always known, in the hands of others from the outset. Individuation is not the first condition of human beings; relationship is. We are precarious, risk-made bodies thrown unavoidably into risk. The story of the Christ-Child – the story of the glory of the Divine handed over into the risk of human life in first-century Palestine – is our story. Even in the midst of the late strategies of an advanced country like the UK, vulnerability and precariousness remains the defining reality of our bodies. Butler summarizes this helpfully when she says:

> I am referring to violence, vulnerability, and mourning, but there is a more general conception of the human with which I am trying to work here, one in which we are, from the start, given over to the other, one in which we are, from the start, even prior to individuation itself and, by virtue of bodily requirements, given over to some set of primary others: this conception means that we are vulnerable to those we are too young to know and to judge and, hence, vulnerable to violence; but also vulnerable to another range of touch, a range that includes the eradication of our being at the one end, and the physical support for our lives at the other.[11]

Grief, it seems to me, entails allowing others in, allowing perhaps the Other in; it is to be in-dwelling, predicating on a certain kind of mutuality. One can of course grieve for those with whom one has a difficult relationship, but in a sense that is predicated on having a relationship, however fraught. I am stunned that Butler, a philosopher with no particular religious

---

11 Butler, *Precarious Life*, p. 31.

commitments, has become fascinated by the notion of being – as bodies – in the hands of others. We are made in and shaped by a kind of radical vulnerability, in community. No matter what strategies we later develop to create illusions of safety, invulnerability, individual and corporate impermeability, and power, we are, first, precarious beings.

Ask most people what they mean by 'precarious', and they will probably say something about physical instability; they may suggest something like 'rickety' or 'liable to fall or collapse'. They may well be familiar with usages like 'a precarious existence', but they may perceive that these derive from the 'physical instability' sense, by the use of metaphor. However, it turns out that the word has quite different origins. The Latin word *precarius* means 'given as a favour', or 'depending on the favour of another person'; the earliest meaning of the English word 'precarious' relates to the idea of being given something – the right to occupy land or to hold a particular position – 'at the pleasure of' another person, who might simply choose to take it back at any time. Indeed, in its Latin origins, *precarius*, there is the implication of entreaty, of obtaining by prayer. To be in a precarious situation is to be dependent on the will of another.

To live precariously in our society is not typically constructed as valuable and significant. Those who have precarious lives are represented as lower down in value; the valued are among those who construct or perform illusions of stability and safety, perhaps through wealth and property. These structures – either national, or personal – work to hide the fundamental precariousness of bodily existence, of how easily we are undone. 'Success' and 'goodness' are so often represented as 'not-precarious'. We even have rhetorics in which the successful will often emphasize their 'self-made-ness' and their lack of dependence on others. Yet Butler and, as I shall suggest, Christian positions want to explore precariousness not as the locus of failure but as a site of value and meaning.

The possibility of grief is a signal of precariousness and vice versa. The centre for this interplay is the body. Gilles Deleuze, drawing on Spinoza, suggests, 'We do not know what the body

9

can do.'[12] To that statement of possibilities I am inclined to add, we often refuse to know or acknowledge what bodies do to each other. It remains one of the abiding moments of various feminisms to insist that we never lose sight of what bodies offer each other: in terms of liberation and injuring and violence. The ground of bodies is dangerous, for it contains the risk of exploitation and violence, and yet it is also a site of holiness in a rich, rich sense. We walk in the midst of the wonder and terror of identity and its limits, its gifted precarity and its remaking. And yet more: as many of you will know, many theorists suggest the body is a disputed site of power relations. The ongoing, often entrenched arguments about the status of trans people, intersex people, people of colour, cis-women and so on, not only among religious people but across political and cultural divides, indicate the disputed status of many bodies. And louring over this are normative bodies or the normative body, typically ordered around concepts of masculinity, power-over and whiteness.

To reiterate: the possibility of grief is a signal of precariousness and vice versa. The centre for this interplay is the body. Why bodies rather than souls or selves or even subjects? Or mind? Part of the answer lies in the way bodies keep us honest, keep us to account, especially around our pastoral praxis and human living. Bodies signal our fragility and precariousness; as matter they expose us to non-negotiable truths – birth, death, the way we are always at risk of trauma. We are so readily torn apart. We find our common ground in bodies. Even as we not unreasonably talk of 'psychic trauma' we are fools if we do not pay attention to how that is represented in and through the body. The theorist Roberta McGrath suggests,

Death is what we most fear in ourselves. This is what lies beneath the skin, what threatens to break through and de-

---

12 Gilles Deleuze, *Lecture Transcripts on Spinoza's Concept of Affect*, p. 7, www.gold.ac.uk/media/images-by-section/departments/research-centres-and-units/research-centres/centre-for-invention-and social-process/deleuze_spinoza_affect.pdf (accessed 20.04.2020).

stroy life. It is our bodies which in the end give up on us ... It is little wonder that we both love and hate the body, and that we project our desire and fear on to others. In the meantime, there are diversionary tactics: we try to contain or at least limit the progress of death by making more humans; we try to thwart death by making objects.[13]

Equally, as the womanist theologian and psychotherapist Phillis Sheppard claims:

> We need to consider 'the body' in the context of a society where certain bodies are exploited to create a desire for commodities, regardless of the need or ability to afford them; where the color of our skin continues to greatly influence our quality of life, our experiences of society, and our economic locations ... where sex and sexuality, used to sell 'entertainment', is infused with violence. We need to hear what the body has to tell us about being created in the image of God.[14]

And, of course, there is goodness in bodies. I say this in resistance to a misunderstanding in so much of patriarchal Christianity which has led to fear of bodies, and of women's bodies and black bodies and queer bodies especially. Our theological panic around flesh has demeaned the body. It has led to so much loss. Western Christianity has not had a good track record around the body, leading many people to believe that Christians hate the body and all its 'filthy' works. In *Dazzling Darkness*, I suggest:

> Bodies stink. Bodies sweat. Bodies decay and wrinkle. Bodies wobble. Bodies are toned, taut systems of cells. Bodies are incredible and beautiful and remarkable. Bodies hold the power to destroy themselves. And, as Janet Morley says, 'The

---

13 Roberta McGrath, *Seeing Her Sex: Medical Archives and the Female Body* (Manchester and New York: Manchester University Press, 2002), p. 10.

14 Phillis Sheppard in Pamela Lightsey, *Our Lives Matter: A Womanist Queer Theology* (Eugene, OR: Pickwick, 2015), pp. 49–50.

bodies of grownups/ come with stretchmarks and scars/ faces that are lived in/ relaxed breast and bellies.'[15]

Bodies are the theatres of our lives.

Surely God has no fear of bodies. This is the truth at the heart of the incarnated God. The idea of God emptying herself into fragile flesh is one of the great shocks of Christian theology. And it is a great affirmation of the goodness of bodily existence – of a god who is prepared to enjoy the company of friends at a wedding, who eats and drinks and weeps at the death of a friend. And even if, theologically, we are inclined to take this embodied God and assert no sin on her part, we must still deal with and embrace the implications of embodiment: physical fragility, bodily changes, living in the emotional complexity of human being. Ultimately this is defined and demonstrated in the Passion of Christ. This is a god so in love with our incarnational fragility that she seeks to redeem us through a willingness to be broken in body. A particular, embodied existence stands for all and, in her faithfulness to love, shows us the way to live.

I wonder if there is a kind of knowing that works only in and through our precariousness: by grief, suffering, by alienation and pain. Patriarchal philosophies have often claimed that knowing things is an intellectual matter. Clearly that is true for many kinds of knowing. But it shows a failure of imagination to suppose that one can truly know love or tragedy at an intellectual level. Sometimes suffering is a kind of practical recognition or perception, mediated through the body. That is to say, it is, for the sufferer, revelatory. It is an expansion of the world, partly constituting a person's correct understanding of her situation as a human being.

The God who steps forward to meet us in the Garden of Possibility is the god of solidarity, who shares our lives, our precarity and vulnerability, the grief and glory of bodies. This god is Love. Yes, Love, but not a love that is soppy, untested. It is Jesus Christ found within and without: the Love that is so

---

15 Rachel Mann, *Dazzling Darkness* (Glasgow: Wild Goose, 2012). p. 88.

outrageous that it becomes a human, fragile and breakable. Easily tortured, damaged and destroyed, but real because of that. We live in extraordinary times when perhaps more than ever we 'allow others in' in fascinating ways. With the death of über-famous figures like David Bowie or George Michael, we see significant outpourings of emotion and grief; their cultural productions and personas have an extraordinarily powerful impact on our bodies as sites of pain; equally, we can be alienated from the bodies and lives around us, in close proximity.[16] We operate receding scales of value, in which we struggle to grieve for and over homeless, economically excluded, asylum-seeking bodies, and so on. I wonder if Christ's precarious glory offers us a way to begin to value again.

---

16 It will be interesting to see how this phenomenon unfolds in a post-Covid-19 world. In a time of social-distancing, perhaps our longing for physical contact may lead to a refiguring of our relationships with those who live on our streets and neighbourhoods. What I don't think will change is our capacity to transfer our love, desire and longing for connection on to those whom we know only via screens, music streaming services and other media. We have a gift for treating 'absences' (for that, for example, is what a film is) as 'presence' and 'intimacy'.

The Glory and Decay of
a Dying Body[1]

The Ordinal

I've lived for the feelings of others,
That's a listening of sorts,

What have I learnt? That self
Is bitumen, black as tar,

Oh, how slowly we flow, oh
How slowly we flow, we crack with age.

I've lived for the feelings of others,
A philosophy of sorts. I've heard

Self give up its final word,
Coughs and whispers in

Hospitals and nursing homes.
Oh, how slowly we flow, oh.[2]

---

1 A section of this chapter, regarding the theology of 'dwelling', was included in Rachel Mann, 'The Priest Attends to the Word: Parish Poetics', in Jessica Martin and Sarah Coakley (eds), *For God's Sake: Re-Imagining Priesthood and Prayer in a Changing Church* (Norwich: Canterbury Press, 2016), pp. 78–91.

2 Rachel Mann, *A Kingdom of Love* (Manchester: Carcanet, 2019), p. 7.

There is something compelling about bodies. I know that some people of faith and of none may find that strange or disconcerting. They may prefer to speak of 'selves' or 'subjects', or even 'souls' and 'minds'. Part of my fascination with bodies is the result of very particular academic training which resists the crushing effects of two and a half thousand years' worth of philosophical thought that privileges patriarchal ideas about subjectivity. Partly, as I indicated in the last chapter, I think to talk of bodies keeps us honest. There is a potency in materiality, or at least in going in search for it. Bodies invite us to be alert to the way in which so much theological and philosophical discourse is inclined to fetishize concepts and ideas. Too readily in European tradition/s, 'mind', 'thought' and 'soul' have been associated with masculinity, power and authority; too often women, as well as those coded as 'non-white' and many others treated as 'subaltern', have been over-identified with the bodily – that is, with changeability, fragility and the labile. There is enormous critical power to be unearthed by attention to the meanings embedded in bodies, positive, negative and otherwise.

For those of us interested in God or ministry or discerning what it means to be a person of faith, careful attention to bodies, to the bodily and so on, has the capacity to break open the riches and terrors of the Divine in extraordinary ways. I am not saying that 'soul' or 'mind' or even 'person' has no traction in the holy warp and weft of a life; far from it. There is always value in wrestling with the soul as a horizon of hope. Since I first came across it in my early twenties, I've always been arrested by Ludwig Wittgenstein's statement in the *Philosophical Investigations*, 'My attitude towards him is an attitude towards a soul. I am not of the opinion that he has a soul.'[3] There is something remarkable about perhaps the key advocate for non-metaphysical philosophy, the man who encourages us to understand the ways language can obfuscate and generate pseudo-philosophical problems, talking about

---

3 Ludwig Wittgenstein, *Philosophical Investigations* (Cambridge: Cambridge University Press, 1988 (1953)), II, IV, p. 178.

'soul'. However, Wittgenstein follows this with an even more remarkable assertion: 'The human body is the best picture of the human soul.'[4]

I have seen bodies in states of glory and states of decay. I know what it is to negotiate the depredations of my own precarious and compromised flesh. To be alongside or with bodies – with souls – in times of hope and suffering and doubt is part of the work of a priest, indeed of much of her most authentic and satisfying work. As I write this, I think of Enid and Anne. Enid was one of my churchwardens when I started my first incumbency, a woman of immense wit, fierce clarity and generosity. If it had been permitted, when she was young, she would have been a priest. When I knew her, she was in her eighties, a widow and close friends with a couple of the women at church, one of whom was Anne. Enid was one of those people one imagines will go on and on for ever with almost undiminished energy.

The week Enid died was an ordinary one, full of the usual mix of meetings, prayer, random pastoral encounters and everyday exhaustion. I'd seen Enid at the Eucharist on the Sunday and she was in as lively form as ever, making plans for her next holiday with her friends. In the middle of the week I was away overnight with a friend; when I came back the next day, I did my usual reflex thing: I checked the Rectory answer-machine. Anne, her close friend, had left a message to say Enid had called an ambulance in the morning with some heart-related problem. There was a second message, left a few hours later, which indicated that Enid had been told she needed surgery, but she was feeling quite positive about it. On the off-chance, and – truth be told – feeling a little guilty that I'd been away when the crisis had hit, I rang Anne to get an update. Anne reported that Enid was now out of surgery and in recovery. She had been told this because she was down as Enid's next of kin. At this point, I felt there was not going to be much more to be done for the evening, so I decided to go and take a bath. It was – in my memory – about 40 minutes later that my phone rang

4 Wittgenstein, *Philosophical Investigations*, p. 178.

again. It was Anne, and Anne had been told that things had taken a turn for the worse with Enid. If Anne wanted to see her to say goodbye she should go to the hospital immediately. I offered her a lift and, having dressed properly in clericals, we went up to the Manchester Royal Infirmary together.

To witness the death of another can be distressing. Our time with Enid was not so much distressing – if this does not sound too pious – but holy and privileged. When we arrived in the recovery room, Enid was surrounded by machinery, her breathing regulated by a ventilator and her body wrapped in an enormous aluminium-style blanket. She was obscured by technology. After establishing with Anne that she was happy for me to be present, a young doctor explained the situation to Anne: Enid was going to die. There was nothing they could do to stop the bleeding. She would die, machinery or not, within the hour. The question was: did Anne prefer to allow Enid to die held together by machines, or would she prefer the medical staff to remove the machinery? If they did, Enid would die within a few minutes. I will never forget how Anne looked at me. Looked to me. The look of someone wrestling with shock and responsibility and the difference between two kinds of decision. For to say, 'No, leave her on the machines' was a decision too.

We were both out of our depth, as all humans are in the face of death, no matter how inevitable. I think we looked at each other without words for what felt like a long time. Anne has always had a gritty, pragmatic grace, a woman who has said to me on many occasions, 'Rachel, tears are the price we pay for loving people.' And each of us, in our own way, loved Enid. I think I might have said, 'Would Enid really wish to go to God surrounded by machines?' We didn't really need to say any more. Anne told the medic to remove the machinery, as I held Anne's hand.

There is nothing to fear in death. At least, that's how it seemed that night, and how it's seemed to me on several occasions when I've had to face my own death. There is a kind of grace that can come to greet us *in extremis*, which removes *timor mortis*. I shall never forget the ritual of the removal of tubes and electronics and machinery. These things had kept

Enid artificially alive and now they were disappearing. Nurses attended her in strange ritual dance, slowly revealing Enid to Anne and me. I was reminded then, as I've been reminded since, of the way they acted as a kind of medical analogue of Maundy Thursday's Stripping of the Altar, where the decorations in the sanctuary are taken away ahead of the austere pain of Good Friday.

The nurses worked silently, switching machines off, removing the ventilator, stripping away the blanket. From behind the power of modern medicine, a body emerged, Enid's body. She came into view, exposed and frail and precariously holding on to mortal life. Anne and I sat down next to her and talked to her, of our love for her, of God's cherishing. I spoke of her faithfulness and we thanked her for all we had received through her grace. The nurses had taken away the marks of medical power and left the altar of her body. And I have never seen her more clearly or more graced as her breathing slowed.

One machine was left attached. It marked the rhythms of her heartbeat, that sign of life and love, of the very centre of our being. Slowly, oh so slowly, as the minutes passed, the pulse dropped: 60 ... 55 ... 40 ... 37 ... 20 ... Anne and I fell silent in Enid's presence, witnesses to something. And Enid was there and not there, and she looked in those final moments so beautiful and at peace. Anne said, 'That's Enid, I can see her now.' And, then, she was gone, and our attitude towards her was towards a soul. Enid's body was the best picture of her soul.

If I ever believed in the modern ideology that 'life is short, so make sure you have and do as much as you can', I do not now. Of course, I want people to have rich and fulfilled lives, with opportunities to encounter life in all its abundance. I'd also like that for myself. However, the belief that such abundance is about having as many experiences and building as many memories as possible strikes me as a very late, very privileged and almost certainly consumerist conception of what it is to be a flourishing, fulfilled body. It is partly predicated on money and disposable time, and may even rely on a conception of the subject as constructed most authentically through pleasure and memory.

To be human, in my view, is to be located. Or perhaps better: to be human is to have to negotiate what it means to be both located and dislocated – to have a sense of place and also to negotiate the shifting realities of being human and Christian. It is one way we can treat with our precariousness. Writing specifically about women's relationship with poetry, Yopie Prins and Maeera Shreiber make a helpful general observation about the etymology of the verb 'to dwell'. They remind us that the notion of 'dwelling' gestures towards 'a process of perpetual displacement, [reclaiming] the wayward etymology of "dwelling" not as a hypothetical house to inhabit but as a verb that also means to go astray, leading us away and unpredictably elsewhere'.[5] In so far as the Church of England remains a parochial community, how we participate and dwell in God's poetics remains – for the most part – a parochial matter. Yet, if the poetic Word's 'dwelling' in the world is contextual, it is also, by its very nature, a place of habitation and a place we creatively go 'astray from'. The 'going astray' is no cause for 'moral' concern – rather, it is the social, cultural and aesthetic condition that leads us into 'the new'. It is in our departures from established meanings, practices and ideas as much as in our traditions that we are faithful to the Word's poetic indwelling.

Theologically, then, Jesus Christ as the incarnated Word of God – fully human, fully divine – represents the definitive reconciliation point between the material and the Divine. God's making, or *poiēsis*, is not to be reduced to the initial creation and on-going sustaining of the world; Christ acts as an icon of re-making and re-creating the world. The Word is before the world, but also participates in the world's redeeming. As St John has it, the Word became flesh and dwelt among us. God's fundamental *poiēsis* indwells the world and remakes it.

---

5 Yopie Prins and Maeera Shreiber, *Dwelling in Possibility: Women Poets and Critics on Poetry*, Reading Women Writing (Ithaca and London: Cornell University Press, 1997), p. 1. In Old English, 'dwellen' means 'to lead astray', developing into 'tarry, stay in place' in Middle English.

In our participation in Christ – in church, in Eucharist, as part of the Body – we participate in that creating, and our material reality is transformed. 'Dwelling' with and in God is both a recapitulation of the world and a going 'astray' from ready-made meanings. But if that is our vocation in community, it is specifically central to that ministry which gathers up those things which make the church 'the church' – the priesthood. And even if we abstract the dimensions of priesthood ('forgiveness and reconciliation' and so on), it is first an incarnated matter. That is, it is 'enfleshed' and located and dwelt within. Incarnated priesthood comprises the set of practices and ways of being that might be said to make up the 'habitus', or the 'warp and weft', of ministry. Participating in 'the poetic' – God's making, our making and the making of others – is part of the proper habitus of ministry. It draws us deeper into relationship with God, the ecclesial community and the world.

Recently, a member of my congregation told me a story that I think, in its truth and simplicity, captures much of the theological potency of my thinking on 'dwelling' and *poiēsis*. This story will stay with me for as long as I have memory. He talked about his dad who was drawing near to death. My friend explained how his mum faithfully visited his dad in his nursing home. They'd been together for over 50 years and, despite his failing health, she would read to him constantly: poetry, Shakespeare, the Bible. My friend said that the last time he'd seen his dad he would still wake up from time to time indicating when he enjoyed a line or an idea. His dad was that sort of man.

However, in recent days, his mum had reported that he had stopped responding. My friend then told me the thing that will stay with me: as his dad faded away, his mum was tempted to try and bring him back, to try and wake him up and get his attention. Then she realized that it would be wrong to try and reclaim him. For it would be interrupting his dad's final task, his final piece of work. He was, as she put it, 'busy'. His body had work to do, and that work was utterly absorbing. That work was dying, and it invited his wife to exercise the grace to let him go. My friend got in touch later that day to say that his father had died. Life drifts from its moorings and it travels homewards.

Our bodies are no mere containers of consciousness. Nor are we mere flesh or meat. We are creatures who dwell in the world and work out our salvation within it. This applies as much to Enid and Anne, my friend's father, me and you. We have work to do, and sometimes that work is dying. Dying can be a kind of making too, of *poiēsis*. Perhaps that way of expressing the point either makes living sound too grand or too prosaic. However, either way, living and dying is a precarious matter, not least because it is an indwelling work of bodies, and of the Body of Christ too. It is a this-worldly matter, which gestures towards eternity and transcendence. It gestures towards hope and the Garden of Resurrection, and the promise of reconciliation. It is where Christ dwells, the one who bears the wounds and who is raised for and to love. In the Body of Christ are all our deaths and all our livings, all our precariousness and all our promise.

3

A Study in the Punctured Body

In his famous book on photography, *Camera Lucida*, the philosopher and literary theorist Roland Barthes invites his reader – or spectator – to consider a striking photograph that shows a war-torn street.[1] The black-and-white photograph, taken in 1979 by Koen Wessing, shows a scene in Nicaragua. The viewer witnesses a street devastated by violence. It is full of rubble and detritus. In the foreground we see three heavily armed soldiers, patrolling the street. They face primarily towards Wessing's camera. Each is poised and alert for trouble. Behind the soldiers we see two nuns walking from (our) left to right across the street. One of them looks in the direction of the camera. The lead nun simply gets on with her business, seemingly without distraction.

In his analysis of this photograph, as well as of others in *Camera Lucida*, Barthes explores a distinction between what he calls the *studium* and the *punctum*. The *studium* (as in study – a seat of learning) represents ordinary knowledge. It is what orientates us and enables us to make sense of and get a grip on the image in front of us. At its most basic, the *studium* consists of conventional images and expectations, the catalogue of imagery already in our heads. It is what orientates us and initially grabs our attention. It is the basic composition of the image. The broken and frightening war-torn street Barthes invites us to consider is not alien to us – even if we find it troubling and distressing – because it is drawn from our conventional representations of war and conflict built up

---

1 Roland Barthes, *Camera Lucida*, trans. Richard Howard (London: Vintage Classics, 2020 (1982)), pp. 28–35.

over the history of photography. It draws on the catalogue of expectations drawn from war photography, from those ghostly daguerreotypes of the American Civil War through to the cratered landscapes generated by carpet bombing in World War Two. When we look at this Venezuelan street scene, even if we have never been in a war zone, we see and recognize a war photo. It has the conventional structures and tropes of much war photography. There are soldiers. There is devastation. Its patterns strangely assure and comfort us, even if war is by its nature troubling.

In contrast, Barthes suggests, this photo also holds within it the *punctum*. The *punctum* consists of those elements in the photo that prick, cut, punctuate, break or wound the *studium*. In anatomy, the *punctum* is the opening of the tear duct. It is also the mark made by a pointed instrument. For Barthes, in his analysis of photography, the visual points or marks that break the conventional 'study' are like so many wounds. It is a sting and a tiny hole. A photograph's *punctum* is that accident that pricks us and bruises us.

In the war photo Barthes considers, the *punctum* is represented by the presence of the nuns. One of them looks in the direction of the soldiers, although she does not engage them via eye contact or words. The other nun simply ignores the soldiers. Barthes suggests that the power or 'adventure' of the photo derives from the co-presence of two discontinuous elements: of soldiers and of nuns. The presence of the nuns breaks or punctures the conventions of war photography and potentially disorientates or even distresses us. At one level, the frame of war is expanded – through the photo we recognize, if we did not before, that war also includes nuns as well as soldiers. More intriguingly, the spectator is invited into new, potentially troubling understandings of the world, of truth and the jarring possibilities of lived reality. As the nun looks towards us, she interrogates us. She asks, perhaps, what right have we to look? Who are we? What kind of person or body is the spectator, us?

Barthes contends that photography has a specific power to hold these jarring intersections of *studium* and *punctum*. Others have criticized him for the elusiveness of examples of *punctum*.

The *punctum* as a place of shock and wounding, it has been suggested, eludes systems of representation: as soon as one seeks to express the *punctum* in language it becomes part of the conventional, the understood – the *studium*. In the setting of this book, I am less interested in Barthes's understanding of the specific demands of photography or the semantic challenges of articulating the *punctum*, the places of puncturing. Almost instinctively, I sense his distinction – always fragile, always precarious and at risk of making the place of wounds the place of conventional knowledge – speaks into the realities of the Divine and of our embodiment and what it means for us to seek to live as sanctified bodies.

I suppose I am saying that in the language of *studium/punctum* one encounters the wound of knowledge, the breaking open of the body, the place of location and dislocation where God's strange otherness is revealed and calls us to make a response. This puncturing makes available, in the wound, new knowledge – new ways of encountering and living the world. I want to suggest that the breaking open of the body – God's and one's own – can be a place where the puncturing, the *punctum*, makes a fuller grasp of the world available. The puncturing opens a wound – *vulnus* – through which new possibilities may flow. The vulnerability may become too much for us. One might bleed out. One might become so exposed that the place of *vulnus* becomes infected. With what? The world? Truth? The Divine? Or perhaps the Divine finds its way to us in the wound. In the body's precarity. How can I articulate this? Perhaps with a story from my own body.

I have had many operations over the past 20-plus years. I have undergone what is commonly called 'sex reassignment' or 'gender confirmation' surgery. That is a significant surgical procedure. I have also had over a dozen surgeries, major or minor, as a result of living with Crohn's disease. Some of the most significant have been to form stomas. Thus far, at different times, I have had two colostomies and two ileostomies. The order of formation runs as follows: a loop or temporary colostomy in 1999, a loop ileostomy (while retaining the loop colostomy) in 2004, a permanent or end colostomy in

2006 and a permanent or end ileostomy in 2008. It is fair to say that my abdomen is rather scarred, not least because of several laparotomies as well as significant scarring from badly healed wounds. As convention has it, one can play chess on my tummy.

For many people there is something quite frightening or distressing about having a stoma or even being near one. It is something associated with ill and old/er – and therefore vulnerable – people. People with colostomy bags are often the butt of jokes. This, arguably, is a very human means of negotiating anxiety and fear, even if it is founded in fear. There is also the simple fact that having 'lips' – a stoma – opened up in one's abdominal wall brings one very close to one's shit. Shit generally disgusts us. It is waste. Its value is unobvious to most of us, most of the time. Its stench is a signal of badness.

When one has a colostomy or ileostomy bag, shit is near and present at all times. One feels its warmth as it oozes out into the bag. Ileostomies work almost constantly and produce faeces of very loose consistency. One can empty the bag ten times a day if it's a bad day. And one has to change the bag regularly, of course. Sometimes when changing a bag, it's impossible not to get shit on your hands. That's how it is much of the time. The smell is vile. Obscene. Those bright red lips look at you, they roll and move constantly, and they pump one's body's waste out. With an ileostomy, the stool is also very acidic. One's own shit corrodes the skin. A stoma is the inside of the body brought outside. It is corrosive material brought into contact with skin.

I want to place the facts of a stoma in the economy of *studium* and *punctum*. Stoma is one way in which the body, in which skin, may be punctured. It is, for the most part, a distressing thing to happen (at least initially). My first stoma was elective, that is, I chose it. I asked for it. I was 29. I adapted to the fact of having lips on my abdomen reasonably quickly. Nonetheless, adaptation to this new reality takes time and sometimes it felt painfully slow. The first time I had to change my bag alone, I wept and fumbled. I thought it would be impossible. I thought my independent life was over. Some people generally struggle to adapt. I remember meeting a man in his thirties who simply couldn't accept this shift in his reality. His only plan was to get rid of the stoma as soon as possible. Once, when I was an in-patient, I remember meeting a young woman of about 17. She was starving herself because it was the only way to stop her stoma working. She was stick-thin and on the verge of being fed via a tube into her veins.

My first ileostomy, formed when I was desperately ill and as an emergency, took me months to accept. Despite being used to having a stoma, this emergency operation was utterly traumatizing. I could barely look at the new stoma. I thought it leered at me. It sprayed shit everywhere. When my colon was later removed in 2008, and my ileostomy became definitive, I also suffered from serious subcutaneous infections. These took over three months to heal. Seaweed was fed into the wounds to heal the deep trauma from the base. I felt like so much poisoned sea.[2]

The body, conventionally, is a site of nine openings. We typically live this body with a kind of ordinary comfort, though the profound shifts of puberty can puncture the *studium*, the body image, of that lived reality. Puberty's wild changes can puncture and disturb the equilibrium of the lived and living body. One has to learn to live one's body in new ways. As a trans person who transitioned in their early twenties, I suppose I've had to learn to live my body in multiple, seemingly strange ways. In addition, as a person with Crohn's, I have had to learn to live with additional openings into my body. I live with insides on the outside. I live with shit and stench, and I have come to know that to accept this reality is not only life-saving but a place of goodness and gift and hope. It is a place, I sense, of *punctum*; of new, potentially troubling understandings of the world, of truth and the jarring possibilities of lived reality. Herein is part of the adventure of the body: of its precarious promise and its fragile hope, which I think is the only hope that

---

2 For a sequence of poems that explores my experience of surgery, trauma and healing, see Rachel Mann, *A Kingdom of Love* (Manchester: Carcanet Press, 2019), pp. 53–7.

should interest us. Why? Because this is the hope God reveals to us in his punctured body.

God himself, in Jesus Christ, becomes the site of puncturing, the *punctum* made flesh. God knows human openings, of course. He knows how the world gets into the body. He knows the places where the costs and pleasures of being mortal issue forth and are received. In Christ, God weeps through *punctum*, the tear ducts. He breathes and speaks and hears and listens. He micturates and defecates. He knows the pleasure of having a penis that can grow hard and squirt semen. And he is pierced upon a cross. In crucifixion, God's body, thereby, becomes a site of five additional openings: the places where nails have pierced skin and bone, and the wound in the side, created by a thrust of a spear. Christ, in his puncturing, is a site of water and blood. If the soldier, in his clumsiness, had pierced the colon or ileum as he thrust his spear up through Christ's body into his lungs and heart, God would also have become a site of stoma.

I trust I say nothing unorthodox. It is the pierced body of God that holds the promise of our full humanity. It is the shock of recognition of our precariousness and our promise. It is the site of reconciliation of humanity to God and God to humanity. It is a site of trauma, grief and wreck. Of *punctum*. And, yet, the mystery is the possibility of hope in the wreckage. The risen body is a punctured body, it is *punctum* that reformulates the adventure – the *aventuren*, the risk of losing, the travel that risks everything – of the human body called into the divine body. Only in the risk of everything lost, only in the 'walk towards' death and breakage, only in the hands of the other, is the fullness of life and human being revealed and discovered.

I think this is the only conception of body that matters in a world on fire, in collapse, in crisis; a world on fire, on fire from within, seemingly against itself; a world where goodness and mercy are under strain, and precariousness is so prevalent that many can no longer appreciate the facts of their fragility. They hanker after walls and impermeable borders. They would make their skin of aluminium and steel, and they would run from the touch of others for no good reason. They would prefer or even seek out what divided Berliners called, in the days of the Wall, *mauerkrankheit* or 'wall-sickness'. For these are not among those who fear touch because of the violence that has been done to them; or because their health status means that touch might kill. These are those who simply want to remain untouched for fear of being changed by the needs and longings of the other. These are those – are us, is me – when we are in the mode of resisting the punctured body of the Living God. It is us when we resist his *punctum* to our late, late unimaginative study of human being.

All this talk of puncturing makes me think of that which is punctured for the sake of revelation: skin. In 1 Corinthians, St Paul suggests that in one individual body there are many members or parts. What is true for the individual body is true also for the Body of Christ. 'Which part am I?' any of us might ask. It is a telling question if we dare to take it seriously. I suspect that many would be drawn to be the rather more glamorous, or noted, parts – brain, heart, lungs; others might be drawn to being limbs or fingers. Some might even want to be the guts. I'm a vain sort of person. There is something appealing for a person with a big ego like me to want to be heart or brains.

However, I wonder if more of us should want to be skin. Skin, that remarkable organ, so readily ignored as an organ until it is damaged. Skin. It is permeable. It is necessary. Destroy too much of one's body's store of it and one cannot live. It provides both a barrier between the inner workings of the body and the wider world, and also offers a profound means of relationship. It is how we touch the world and how it meets us. Its haptic possibilities are manifold: blessing, destruction, tenderness. It is a key way the body breathes and regulates temperature, allowing moisture to escape from our bodily system; this regulation happens without our conscious thought. We give off heat and life and salt. Through our skin we feel the cold; we feel the bleak possibilities of winter encroach and close in, and through it we sense also the opening out of the world's possibilities through sex and pleasure, athletic prowess and so on. In the bright sunshine of a March day, one feels the fresh possibilities of spring begin to open out.

Skin matters. It is politicized and coded. Different shades of skin are – consciously or unconsciously – assigned value. When I lived in Jamaica nearly 30 years ago, there was, in the professions, a profound cultural bias towards whiteness: the darker one's skin the less likely one was to be employed in a bank or other middle-class settings. Indeed, relative 'lightness' of skin shade has, for some models, actors and singers, been a route into wider 'white-focused' cultural success and acceptance.[3] Equally, it should come as no surprise that in some slang the sex industry is known as the skin trade. The word 'skin' holds within it a complex, fascinating and sometimes troubling range of significations.

Our skin holds all of the stories that we shall ever have, in this life anyway. Our scars and wounds, and our triumphs and joys too. As Janet Morley wisely acknowledges, the bodies of grown-ups come with scars and stretch marks.[4] Life requires that skin loses the downy perfections of infancy and be tested and broken by the troubles and possibilities of living. Those who are tempted to hide behind make-up or plastic surgery can only partially disguise the decay of their skin. There is a kind of withering which not even the finest make-up artist or plastic surgeon can disguise. And then, as one enters one's twilight days, skin can create the appearance of being so thin it seems translucent. One's skin may become covered in 'liver spots', which a friend of mine calls 'hepatic camouflage'.

Our skin tells the tales of our loves and losses, the nature and shape of our work, and the way – the often sinful way – society encodes who it says we are. It opens us to the possibilities of blessing and the terrible facts of the violence held within our species. It is a place of puncturing and *punctum*. We are punctured and pierced, as God is punctured and pierced. He

---

3 Consider, for example, the breakout success of Vanessa Williams, the first African-American winner of Miss America, actor and singer. The superb podcast *You Must Remember This* (about Classic Hollywood and its tropes) devotes an episode to Williams and the way her lighter skin colour proved a way for her to breakthrough into the 'affections' of White America.

4 Janet Morley, *All Desires Known* (London: SPCK, 1988), p. 113.

is punctured for our transgressions. We are so often punctured by the transgressions of a structurally sinful world.

We are members of one Body. We are sojourners on a fragile earth. Let us dare to want to be God's skin, ready to be pierced for the sake of hypocrites and fools; ready to be an open border for grace; ready to bless one another and more: to live and die and live-again for a ruinous world. Let us be ready to touch heaven and be touched by heaven in ordinary, stooped to earth in God's new creation. We are many,[5] and, as one body, we dream. It is late and the world is old and weary. Fires burn and floods wash away story and hope. And perhaps we are no longer young, and we look around us and pray that someone else, anyone, will have sufficient energy to take care of the work of loving, and the holding fast, and the practice of hospitality and blessing; to dare to be God's Body punctured for the world and – crucially – daring to expose that world for its violence and cruelty, and call it into another way of life.

---

[5] Though, if one is an Anglican, perhaps it seems we are not so many as once we were!

4

To Risk the Womb with Gladness

It can be very difficult for any of us to accept the fundamental precariousness of our bodies, their deep materiality and limitation. Perhaps this is especially the case when we are young. While I know many young people with challenging and sometimes limiting conditions, many of us when young encounter our bodies as seemingly eternal, as unstoppable locations of love, energy and wonder. Many of us, though not all, know the body's capacity for seemingly boundless delight.

Of course, in truth, our bodies are frail. We are frail. If we live long enough, our bodies will be unpicked and decay – every sinew, every piece of connective tissue, will unravel. Whether we live a long time or a brief time, the marrow of our bones shall dry and return to dust. That's what we do. That's part of the code of us. Sometimes, in the middle of the night, I wake – in a kind of echo of that pre-modern practice of first and second sleep – and I'll simply lie there in the dark. As I lie in that warm, dark womb of bedroom, of bed, listening to the hush of cars heading into or out of the city, I think about this stuff; about how all creatures of womb are creatures of tomb too. And I do not find it a dreadful thought.

The Hebrew word for 'compassion' is *rachuwm*. It is taken from the root word *rechem*, which means 'womb'. When I became aware of the connection between womb and compassion, I felt I had encountered something of the structure of God's first language. I felt as if something of the world's substrate was revealed. Of course, even as I say that, I want to be careful. Too often, in a patriarchal culture, 'womb' – full of 'feminine' inflexion, of 'female' or 'feminine' space – has been coded negatively. For, on patriarchal readings, the 'womb' as a metonym for 'woman' exposes women to the risk of being coded as 'hysterical'. This is the world in which, as the old patriarchal claim has it, the womb wanders about a woman's body, making her mad or unreliable or unsafe; a realm where to feel compassion is problematic and risky. Precarious.

Other readings are possible. The connections between womb and compassion also invite us to read God, the God of compassion and mercy and love, differently. This is God as womb-like and as womb-bearer. This is the God who feels for us in her womb. She suffers the suffering of her children in her womb. She holds us in mercy, love and pity. If modern technologies have, in many ways, demythologized wombs – we have the means to look through the abdominal wall and witness the growth of foetuses and place them clearly in technological time and space – there remains a theological potency in a vision of the Divine caught up in the fecundity and cost of compassion, of the compassionate womb. This is not only the God who enters enfleshment through a human womb but the God who has the character of womb itself.

This picture of God is, I think, an invitation to participate in one of the most hopeful horizons of precariousness. As indicated in my previous comments on patriarchal culture, I am conscious that 'womb' as a traditional icon of 'femininity' has been tied up in the language of fear: fear of female power and reproduction, but also of 'femininity' as both dangerously fragile and harbinger (indeed the producer) of death. For wombs not only bring life but also expel the baby out into mortality and limit. As metaphor – noting of course that the root word *metapherein* holds notions of 'carrying' or 'bearing' across – 'womb' can simultaneously represent fecundity and barrenness, life and death.[1] Mary, the Blessed Mother, the one who bears or carries Christ, bears the Divine into death and limit and precariousness. She does so via 'womb', that icon of precariousness.

---

1 *Meta* implies 'over' or 'across', while *pherein* implies 'to carry' or 'bear'.

Womb, then, has so often acted as a metonym for femininity. Conceptually, it can be deployed to suggest that a woman *qua* woman is never truly able to be herself alone. For, according to this line of thought, what defines a woman is ultimately her fecundity – her capacity to reproduce. It is in pregnancy, birth, childrearing and their possibilities that her identity is defined. Unlike a man – who is the icon of independent action and a subjectivity that is performed on the public stage – women are, in patriarchal contexts, domestic, relational subjects. Their identity is never complete in itself. A woman's identity is double, for it is defined by the children she produces and nurtures. Even in the womb, the growing foetus is not to be simply identified with or be reduced to the mother. And yet, both materially and representationally, the foetus/baby is derived from the mother's cells and being. Her flesh weaves and reformulates the becoming of the child's flesh. In birthing the child, part of her enters the world and separates from her.

Sociologist Deborah Lupton has brought out the significance of this 'doubled' reading of women in medical discourse. In this sphere, 'doubleness' is represented in the way women's bodies are coded as crucial both for healthy foetuses/babies, yet are somehow separate from them. Thus, she notes how women are expected to have a healthy lifestyle to ensure that the baby is healthy. She says:

> [This extends] to the moment of conception and even before. Women are now advised not to drink alcohol or smoke cigarettes ... some doctors ... even suggest that a woman *planning* to fall pregnant should be responsible and prepare their body.[2]

However, as Lupton further notes, 'the pregnant woman is increasingly portrayed as separate to and the adversary of her own pregnancy/foetus'.[3] This she illustrates with a story from

---

2 Deborah Lupton, *Medicine as Culture: Illness, Disease and the Body*, 3rd edn (New York, NY: Sage Publications, 2012), p. 167.
3 Lupton, *Medicine as Culture*, p. 166.

Australia regarding unborn babies suing mothers, noting that the story included 'a photograph of a foetus encased in the amniotic sac, seemingly floating in space, a self-contained and apparently self-sufficient individual separate from the maternal body'.[4]

However, for all its patriarchal traces and problems, the God of womb – the one who is unafraid of womb and who finds her being in and through womb – is not to be dismissed. She is the one who knows precariousness, vulnerability and the body as gift. She is the one who can save us, in Christ. This is the God who, as I read it, is prepared to enter what might be called *Khôra*. This term, which was taken up by feminist philosopher Julia Kristeva, draws on Plato's use of the term in *The Timaeus*. In Plato's classical context, *Khôra* – meaning 'space' – was the territory of the polis outside the city proper. It is the 'beyond', the place beyond obvious rule and rules. As Kristeva develops the term, it represents the symbolic outside, the place of the Other. It is the place where meaning is not yet regulated. It is dangerous and questionable space. And, because it is a place where meaning can be questioned, formed and reformed, it may yet be a place for the positive disruption of established meaning.[5]

If one claims or reclaims the womb's wildness and strangeness in positive terms, as a place of making and creating, then womb may come to represent not only an interrogation of patriarchal ideas of meaning but might open space for new possibilities to be birthed. Womb is dark and beyond sight. It is dark and magical as a cave, and new things come to birth there. God is unafraid of that place.[6] If *Khôra* cannot ever quite escape its relationship with a world that demands Order and Regulation, it offers a space for a kind of fecund possibility.

---

4 Lupton, *Medicine as Culture*, p. 166. The story was taken from the Sydney *Sunday Telegraph*, 13 June 1993.

5 Julia Kristeva, *Revolution in Poetic Language*, trans. Margaret Waller (New York, NY: Columbia University Press, 1984).

6 I've always rather loved the Orthodox belief that Jesus was born in a cave.

This is a space that resists patriarchal rules, in which new meanings and possibilities can be generated.

In short, the God of compassion – the one who both models womb and enters womb in the salvation of the world – is unafraid of what Margrit Shildrick has called the 'leaky body'.[7] Christ is made of fragile flesh. He knows dependency and relationship. He knows the leakiness of bodies. He knows we are water and blood and mucus and mess from the outset and that it is good. We are mess as much as we are ever ordered and neat form. He knows that we hold the possibility of 'meat', of being torn apart and decay, within our beauty. From the outset, in his formation, the One Who Saves is never himself alone, never separate and discrete. He is held in body and amniotic sac. And, though he knows the reality – the reality we all know – of being pushed out of the relational womb into the separation of a fragile and frightening world, this is no God who comes down from heaven in a chariot or is simply an avatar of a Greek god. He begins in dependency and grows in the company of humanity. He is nurtured by his mother and learns from her. Mary, as the one who sings the Magnificat, is the one who surely teaches him to speak the Beatitudes.

Childbearing – and, by implication, motherhood and the bodies of mothers – has been represented as precarious and problematic. Certainly, in many periods in history, marked by unsanitary conditions or lack of appropriate care, it has been risky to carry a child and give birth. Thank God that healthcare and birth-care has improved. However, I think it is also important to interrogate how this precariousness has been encoded theologically and culturally. If precarity is part of being human and a place utterly known by the Divine, I see no reason why it cannot be a place of discovered holiness and glory and hope too. The challenge is to articulate this relational, interdependent precarious hope in such a way that

---

7 See Margrit Shildrick, *Leaky Bodies and Boundaries: Feminism, Postmodernism and (Bio)Ethics* (London: Routledge, 1997), and Margrit Shildrick, *Embodying the Monster: Encounters with the Vulnerable Self* (London: Sage Publications, 2002).

claims space for liberation and human dignity. This is tricky: one has to negotiate layers of negative cultural accretion about women, which either over-defines their bodies as – at best – patriarchal agents defined by 'child-bearing', 'motherhood' and 'fertile wombs' or – at worst – the means by which fragility, death and limit enter the world.

This cultural negativity about precariousness – read through the work of the womb – is at least as old as the Bible. Eve, Mother-All, the Life-Mother, has traditionally been read as the recipient of womb-centred punishment for giving Adam the forbidden fruit to eat: she is condemned to suffer the trauma of agonizing childbirth. In Genesis 3.16, God says, 'Unto the woman he said, I will greatly multiply thy sorrow and thy conception; in sorrow thou shalt bring forth children; and thy desire *shall be* [my italics] to thy husband, and he shall rule over thee.' The definitive loss of Eden is constructed through the disobedience, foolishness and affective weakness of women.[8] The innocence and simplicity of Eden – its seeming absence of struggle, strife and precarity – is underlined by the post-Edenic reality in which mothers are condemned to pain and trauma in childbirth.[9] Outside Eden is death and precariousness.

These cultural accretions are not merely religious. Anxieties about precarious and dangerous 'femininity' coded through the image of the womb and women's reproductive power have the patina of science and medicine too. The womb has been represented as the organ that generates malady for women. It has been read as the organ that generates sickness through the pain of menses, but also through the process that is supposed to define a woman: pregnancy (whether in terms of sickness during pregnancy or the pain of childbirth). As Deborah Lupton concludes, 'In the nineteenth and early twentieth centuries, menstruation and pregnancy were treated as abnormal – as

---

8 See Genesis 3.1–7.

9 As many will know, Adam as ur-man is condemned to a life of toil. Many women will want to remind audiences that their experience has been that men have so ordered the world that they have had to take on the vast majority of the labour, more broadly understood, as well as maternal labour. This includes domestic and emotional labour.

sicknesses rather than normal bodily functions. Women were seen as being controlled by their uterus and ovaries.'[10]

---

10 Lupton, *Medicine as Culture*, p. 141. Lupton acknowledges that the emergence of 'hysteria' – a term derived from the Greek for 'womb' – was a 'clear example of the way in which medically defined and documented illnesses are embedded in social, political and historical conditions'. Lupton, p. 141. The over-identification of pregnancy with abnormality and hysteria is no mere nineteenth-century matter. The use of pregnancy as a qualifier in behaviour – even when this qualifier seems utterly irrelevant – can be seen in this example from November 2016: BBC, 'Pregnant Driver Reverses Off Ramsgate Harbour Wall', BBC Online, www.bbc.co.uk/news/uk-england-kent-37880394 (accessed 05.11.2016).

Equally, Roberta McGrath's study of medical representations of women's fertile bodies since the seventeenth century reiterates the patriarchal imperatives that subject women to the male gaze. By the nineteenth century, there were extensive textbooks on women's bodies whose visual representations over-identified women with the womb. Works like William Hunter and Jan Van Riemsdyke's *Anatomy of the Human Gravid Uterus Exhibited in Figures* (1774) created detailed, lavish and fetishized representations of women's bodies and their seeming failings. Cited in Richard Barnett, *The Sick Rose: Disease and the Art of Medical Illustration* (London: Thames & Hudson, 2014), pp. 32–3.

Stephen T. Asma's popular work on the historiography of monsters reminds us that, with the emergence of modern science, the monstrous was medicalized as an effect of wombs, vaginas and female pelvises. He notes how, as early as the sixteenth century, the French surgeon Ambroise Paré moved the discourse on 'birth-defects' from the supernatural to the natural realm. Paré suggests that 'the narrowness or smallness of the womb' is a cause of monsters. Stephen T. Asma, *On Monsters: An Unnatural History of Our Worst Fears* (Oxford and New York: Oxford University Press, 2009), p. 146.

As McGrath suggests, drawing on Latour, 'women's bodies, once they have been inscribed or turned into representation, are easier and safer to look at; they are easier and safer to order, move, preserve or destroy, to take out and put away'. Roberta McGrath, *Seeing Her Sex: Medical Archives and the Female Body* (Manchester and New York: Manchester University Press, 2002), p. 10. See also, Bruno Latour, *Pandora's Hope: Essays on the Reality of Science Studies* (London and Cambridge, MA: Harvard University Press, 1999).

The fecund body, then, becomes fetishized as life-giver and yet dangerously precarious and fragile. Indeed, within the realm of art and

When women's bodies are fetishized as defined by womb, maternity and so on, the fecund body always works as a trace, a reminder of something else: the mother's body.[11] In short, a woman's body is never simply itself alone. It always signifies beyond itself and its first iteration/representation is as 'the mother's body', fecund, yet deathly and sickly. In so far as it is reduced to representations of reproduction – the womb – the female body is always represented as doubled. For not only is 'womb' one step away from 'tomb', but woman is represented in terms of her children. Even as she produces new life, that life is not her own. But there are further significations. The fact of birth is a fundamental marker of the reality of mortality.

Natality is a ground of masculine fear of death and, ultimately, of women. Indeed, Elisabeth Bronfen argues that 'the pictorial representations of dead women became so prevalent in eighteenth and nineteenth century European culture that by the middle of the latter century this topos was already dangerously hovering on the periphery of cliché'.[12] The female body

_____

the discourses of medicine, the female body lives a double life. This shouldn't surprise us. Fetishes – religious, sexual, cultural – hold this doubleness within them. They are always both themselves and represent something else. A person who finds stiletto shoes erotic both acknowledges the fact that these are just shoes, but also lives in the acknowledgement that they gesture beyond themselves. At the same time, there is a disavowal of the banal reality of the shoes; they have become a symbol of something more powerful and significant than is obvious in the particular object. Being in the presence of the fetish is always dangerous and exciting because its symbolic authority always threatens to overwhelm the mundane.

11 Lupton, *Medicine as Culture*, p. 13.

12 Elisabeth Bronfen, *Over Her Dead Body: Death, Femininity, and the Aesthetic* (Manchester: Manchester University Press, 1992), p. 3. Literary representations of the deathly fecundity of feminine bodies abound in the nineteenth century. Gothic novel *Frankenstein* has Mary Shelley turn a male surrogate, Victor Frankenstein, into a new Eve, whose womb is a 'workshop of filthy creation'. In *Wuthering Heights*, Catherine Earnshaw dies in childbirth; her presence remains in the novel as a haunting spectre louring over proceedings. In Gaskell's *Mary Barton*, while Mary is still a young girl, her mother dies in childbirth along with the baby. Crucially, this death is constructed around Mary

becomes both the site of trauma and a traumatic sight. It inspires dread. Elisabeth Bronfen argues that death and femininity, the two enigmas of western culture, are bound together in the concept of castration: the horror for the masculine-constructed subject is in seeing the mother as a castrated version of its own body, who must be mastered if subjectivity is to be assured and achieved.[13] McGrath argues:

> The terror woman inspires derives from the way in which only she gives life, thus starting the individual's more or less lengthy dance with death. The navel, as Bronfen points out, is a scar which never quite heals. Woman is a one-way street.[14]

Visually, the fullness of a woman's pregnant belly, near full term, might be read as akin to a dead body's internal organs bloated and swollen by death gases,[15] the symptoms of ovarian cancer or, in a time of anxiety about 'fat' and body image, as a sign of mistreating the body. In a patriarchal, scopic economy, the fecund body simply looks sick. Again, McGrath reminds us:

> When anatomists began to study the female skeleton in greater detail, it was caught in an already existing web of beliefs about the body of a woman. Unsurprisingly, the female pelvis became the object of obsessive study, which always revealed the same thing: women were not only different from men, but also less than them. Anatomists found out what was already known: woman was malformed.[16]

Barton Snr's grief about her sister Esther's disappearance. Esther, it later becomes clear, had disappeared because she had lost her virtue and fallen into prostitution.

13 Bronfen, *Over Her Dead Body*, pp. 32–5.

14 McGrath, *Seeing Her Sex*, p. 112.

15 Post-battle images of bloated bodies were especially common during the American Civil War. See, for example, John Banks, 'John Banks's Civil War Blog', http://johnbanks.blogspot.co.uk/2016/03/antietam-details-in-gardners-iconic.html (accessed 05.11.2016).

16 Bronfen, *Over Her Dead Body*, p. 3.

The female body, then, was constitutionally ill and damaged; not necessarily even fit for the productive work of baby-making it was assigned in a culture increasingly obsessed with manufacture and industrial processes: 'woman did not give birth, but was delivered of a child. A poorly constructed pelvis or an inefficient uterus were mechanical deficiencies that hindered or prevented the extraction of what was literally a vital commodity.'[17] In short, the pelvis became a metonym for femininity: malformed, necessary, but weak and dangerous.

The very condition of the fecund body under patriarchy, then, is fallenness. To repeat Shildrick's point, 'the very sign of fertility, the menses, has been regarded as evidence of women's inherent lack of control of the body and, by extension, of the self'.[18] This way of stating the fallenness of femininity reiterates the double bind of feminine subjectivity under patriarchy. This double bind also operates at the level of the body's representation: the fecund body of the mother or potential mother is fetishized as the feminine ideal, yet the female body is constructed as unstable, fragile and dangerous. To fall for woman is simply to be a fecund woman. To be representable as a female body is already to be deformed, less and defective.

Of course, one of the mainstays of patriarchal representations of women's fecund bodies as fallen, damaged and deathly is the rhetoric of Christianity. As Mary Colleen M. Conway's study on the construction of gender in the Bible suggests, from early Christianity onwards, subjectivity in Christianity was constructed in terms of mastery.[19] She argues that hegemonic masculinity runs through classical and New Testament writings. It is constructed around 'mastery over non-men', a

---

17 McGrath, *Seeing Her Sex*, p. 100 and p. 71. See also: Andrea Henderson, 'Doll-Machines & Butcher-Shop Meat: Models of Childbirth in the Early Stages of Industrial Capitalism', *Genders* 12.4 (1991), pp. 100–19.

18 Shildrick, *Leaky Bodies*, p. 34.

19 Colleen M. Conway, 'The Construction of Gender in the New Testament', in Adrian Thatcher (ed.), *The Oxford Handbook of Theology, Sexuality and Gender* (Oxford: Oxford University Press, 2015), pp. 222–38 (p. 233).

masculinity that must always be proven in competitive ways. It is a moral value in conflict with effeminacy and the 'weakness' or 'softness' of femininity. It is an anxious concept that depends on asserting that it is 'not-femininity'. Furthermore, Aristotelian biology had a profound impact on Christian thinking about women's bodies in both the patristic and medieval eras. If Christian writers found biblical warrant for male hegemony in stories like that of Adam and Eve, St Thomas Aquinas's claim in the *Summa Theologica* that women are 'failed men' and merely the passive cause in reproduction was undoubtedly drawn from Aristotle.[20]

This account of womb as metonym for fallenness or death or weakness or sickness can seem overwhelming. How is it possible to locate hope, love and faith in this remarkable relational space which culture has so often coded as negatively precarious? For surely it is possible to reclaim the precarious from perdition, isn't it? Of that I'm sure. Certainly, for any number of reasons, 'masculinity' – men, maleness, those coded as male, however you want to express it – has always been able (via violence, power, privilege) to claim priority or 'first place', leaving the rest of us to play catch-up. In claiming their first-place, men are able to derive their legitimacy through divine warrant.

The very opening of Genesis creates the impression that men come first: the masculine-coded God creates a man from dust, bypassing the need for a womb. He claims 'feminine' power to make life unto himself, treating himself as *sui generis*. Woman, as help-meet, is then pulled from the dust-man's body.[21] Finally, the man – who has been given the power of naming – proclaims that his help-meet is woman and is 'flesh of my flesh, bone of my bone'. In this economy, the precarious, fertile

---

20 For a study of medieval Christian theologies of gender, see Ruth Mazo Karras, 'Reproducing Medieval Christianity', in *The Oxford Handbook of Theology, Sexuality and Gender*, pp. 271–86. For an analysis of the 'failed men'/'One Sex' theory, see Adrian Thatcher, *Redeeming Gender* (Oxford: Oxford University Press, 2016), Part 1, Section 2.

21 See Genesis 2.7, 18, 21–24.

world of the womb becomes a secondary matter, subject to the rule of Adam.

This picture of the male God avoiding womb in order to make from dust and dust alone can seem intractable. How is it possible to locate the womb in God? However, as many feminist scholars have drawn out, this masculinist picture is not the only reasonable take on the biblical text.[22] The representation of God as male is profoundly flawed. The first creation narrative holds both male and female pronouns for God. God's Spirit is definitively feminine. Equally, the Adam – the earth creature, *ha'adam* or human creation made from dust – is in Hebrew most properly rendered as 'it'. Its identity holds all meanings within it – male, female, neuter – and it is only in the division of the earth creature that the human persons are called 'man' and 'woman' for the first time. As Wil Gafney helpfully indicates, the concept of 'helper' in English has subaltern connotations – 'a helper is often of lower status than the one being helped'[23] – but this implication does not necessarily hold in biblical Hebrew. *Ezer* is a mighty helper and is drawn from the materiality of the earth creature. Though typically translated as 'rib', the *tzela* is a side, not a rib. There is a rabbinic tradition that suggests that *ha'adam* was divided in two. The 'Adam' is in two bodies, the woman (*Ishshar*) and the man (*Ish*).[24]

Equally, it is possible to bring pressure to traditional representations of Eve or *Chavah*'s 'punishment' for disobedience. As Gafney indicates, the biblical text indicates that 'many and great will be the woman's work (not pain) and her conceptions (not full-term pregnancies or live births). Childbearing will be difficult, hard work. There will be pain, and there will

---

22 See, for example, Athalya Brenner (ed.), *A Feminist Companion to Genesis* (Sheffield: Sheffield Academic Press, 1997 (1993)); Phyllis Trible, *God and the Rhetoric of Sexuality* (Minneapolis, MN: Fortress Press, 1978); Wil Gafney, *Womanist Midrash: A Reintroduction to the Women of the Torah and the Throne* (Louisville, KY: Westminster John Knox Press, 2017).

23 Gafney, *Womanist Midrash*, p. 21.

24 Gafney, *Womanist Midrash*, p. 24.

be desire.'[25] She also indicates that there are powerful grounds in Hebrew to render '[Adam] shall rule over you' as 'he shall rule with you'.

In the case that Gafney makes, and that many of us know at the level of our bodies, in the world delineated by the Bible there will be pain and there will be desire. Childbearing will be difficult, hard work. There will, then, be a reality which has been lived by countless people across millennia. I've never been entirely convinced that the myth of Eden was ever set up as a paradise on earth in the first place. As Lyn Bechtel notes, 'if the garden represents a "paradise", it should, by definition, be devoid of binary opposition and have only life, goodness, permanence and prosperity'.[26] This myth unfolds a shifting and emergent context where new realities emerge within the narrative, including the emergence of gender. The earth creature – the human being that holds all human beings – is formed out of the womb of the earth, the good dust, the good earth. Out of the fertile, fragile, precarious materiality of the earth comes the human, made by God, who is male and female and neither. And childbearing will be hard work, for God and for Eve. It will be precarious and good. Crucially, it is from the outset – from the outset of the human creation – relational. It is not a story of the male God making a man for himself and a woman for the man's pleasure and procreation.

Is it a terrible thing for a priest to confess that as a woman poet I rather delight in Eve's disobedience? Eve's disobedience strikes me as symbolically significant, an act of resistance to her designated role, a refusal to have her meaning totally constrained by Adam and the 'Father figure', God. Indeed, I'm tempted to suggest that Eve becomes an icon for women and

---

25 Gafney, *Womanist Midrash*, p. 25.

26 Lyn M. Bechtel, 'Rethinking the Interpretation of Genesis 2.4B—3.24', in Brenner (ed.), *A Feminist Companion*, pp. 77–118 (p. 79). See also: 'Why has God placed a tree for discernment of good and bad and a snake of evil and death in this paradise? Or if the woman is responsible for bringing evil and death into the world, why is she given the honorable and positive name *'hawwâ*/Eve/Life, mother of all living ... et al.'.

queer poets; for all those who attempt to wrestle not only with language, but seek to rework the inherited possibilities of sign and symbol and word. For, if Eve has so often been represented as the acme of falsehood, of naughtiness, then there is a sense in which she ironically makes poetry possible. She breaks the power of Adam who determines what words mean. She rebels against a creation constructed around a figure who can point at objects and things and persons and say, 'This is x', this is the literal truth. Eve's disobedience and falsehood brings metaphor into the world. In breaking the simple picture of 'this is how things and words relate', she makes metaphor – the transfer of a word into a semantically different, though similar realm – possible. She opens out the world. She opens out the world not only to the delights of language, but to the possibility of life. She is the risk-taker and risk-maker. She shows forth the precarious boldness of the Living God. It is time we stopped traducing her.

5

The Gift and Wound of Relationship

There is an old Jewish story about a hardworking farmer who is blessed with a visit by God and offered three wishes as a sign of good fortune. The wishes come with one simple condition: whatever he wishes for, God will bless his neighbour with double. The farmer accepts God's gracious offer and asks for 100 cattle. When God provides them, he is delighted until he sees the 200 cattle God has given to the farmer's neighbour. Nonetheless, the farmer moves on to his second wish. He asks for 100 acres of land, and again is thrilled until he sees that God has given his neighbour 200 acres. Rather than feeling joy at his good fortune, the farmer could not control his jealousy that his neighbour had received double what he had. So, he presented God with his third and final wish: that he be blinded in one eye. And God wept.

It is possible – from certain points of view – to have a little too much relationship. What I mean is, given that most works of violence are committed in domestic contexts or in familial settings or among those known to us, it is not unreasonable to suggest that too much time in the company of those with whom we are close is dangerous. It is possible for resentments and jealousies to build up. Furthermore, it can be difficult to be joyous about the blessings that can be showered on other people, even those whom we love and respect. We may even want to punish them or cut them dead. Crucially, we can fail to see the blessings we've received and be thankful for them. Instead, like the farmer in the old story, we can concentrate too jealously on the perceived blessings given to others. In doing so, we are as mean to ourselves as to others.

I think the greatest cost in the Christian life is the call to be in the hands of others. To be in mutual trust, recognition and love. That is, to live in community. As someone who has, like most of us, been overly formed in an individualistic, self-directed and arguably excessively capitalistic culture, perhaps I feel extra terror when confronted with the word 'community'. Certainly, as someone trained in the linguistic philosophy tradition, I want to unpack and interrogate the word. What on earth does it gesture towards? Does it, for example, simply mean a group of individuals living in more or less loose affiliation with one another, bounded by rules? Does it gesture towards a deep, common foundation in shared values and virtues, tested over time and place by shared practices? Does it even mean a kind of mutual indwelling, where persons live in and through one another, as in a body?

At the same time, however, I don't question the Christian invitation into community. I'm inclined to read this as an invitation into finding oneself in living, formational relationship in the midst of and company of God and neighbour. The starting-point of Christian life is not so much the individual but the defining community of the Living God, three-yet-one. If that is too abstract, the grounding is found in Christ. He knew that the heart of the fully human life could be captured in his summary of the Law: 'Thou shalt love the Lord thy God with all thy heart, and with all thy soul, and with all thy strength, and with all thy mind; and thy neighbour as thyself.' Love is placed at the centre, and love in the face of the other – God, neighbour, and perhaps especially oneself – is so difficult to recognize.

In his extraordinary book about the cost of love, W. H. Vanstone writes, 'Where the object of love is truly an "other", the activity of love is always precarious.'[1] I suppose, in the first instance, one most readily relates to this truth in relation to one's love affairs and relationships. The fact of the matter is that I've had very few significant ones in my life, and they've

---

1 W. H. Vanstone, *Love's Endeavour, Love's Expense* (London: Darton, Longman & Todd, 2007 (1977)), p. 46.

all been quite intense. I think the ones that have really mattered have been an education in the wonder of otherness and the extraordinary cost of community and relationship. The most significant relationship in my life lasted twelve years and when it ended it took me four years to properly recover, if recover is the right word. I can see now that it was right for that relationship to end, though I didn't want that to happen at the time. Sometimes relationships run their course. The only way we can grow deeper into God is by letting go of that relationship, before all that has been good in it is lost. I often think about the gift of having known the person I loved – how they always exceeded any conception I had of them. I knew them as well as I've known anyone, and I think they knew me as well as anyone ever has or shall. However, they will always remain a mystery. We are mysteries to each other and mysteries to ourselves. Only in God are we fully known, and we have such limited purchase on ourselves. We are creatures who live such bewildering and busy lives that even in those moments when we glimpse a little of ourselves, we doubt it.

For as much as one might wish to take hold of the Christian invitation to find oneself and others in the gift of the Living God – his body – we remain creatures negotiating separateness. In the last chapter, I reflected on how Christ, as much as any of us, is formed in and with the body of another. In the womb of Mary, Christ is woven into life. For Christ as much as the rest of us, life begins in community, but he also knew what it is to be cast out, ejected; we have to be born in order to live and respond to the call to live for others. For all its necessity, it is a separation and, as we grow, we discover the depth of the separation.

Again, Vanstone captures the profundity and pathos that can be generated in the unavoidable gap between different and separate bodies, selves and people, and their desire for and call to love:

> Between the self and the other there always exists, as it were, a 'gap' which the aspiration of love may fail to bridge or transcend … Herein lies the poignancy of love, and its potential

47

tragedy. The activity of love contains no assurance or certainty of completion: much may be expended and little achieved.[2]

In George Eliot's great novel *Middlemarch*,[3] the idealistic parson Camden Farebrother falls in love with blunt, strong-willed Mary Garth. However, inexplicably and yet very humanly, Mary prefers the essentially useless and feckless Fred Vincy. Farebrother is left in the painful position – in the midst of his love, perhaps because of his love – of helping Fred to win Mary's hand. Simply because Farebrother loves Mary, there is no guarantee that such love will be requited.

Could what we experience as love – in its various forms, from the erotic to the filial to the sacrificial – be *love* if it were assured and safe and secure at every point? If precariousness was redacted out? For Vanstone, the answer is no. In Vanstone's words, 'Love proceeds by no assured programme.'[4] Indeed, there is a profoundly improvisatory structure to love. I think 'improvise' is the right word in this context. In Latin it has implications of 'unforeseen', of 'unstudied' and 'not prepared beforehand'. It resists the programmatic. I am not suggesting that there is no intentionality or structure to our loving relationships; rather, they are not reducible to technique or system, not least because they unfold in the realm of the human and therefore the mysterious. Loving relationship requires a sense that the other holds mystery and agency. They exceed our temptations to want control or predictability, and vice versa. Love is adventurous and open-textured.

In this regard I am intrigued by what Vanstone says about the 'precariousness of love's activity' in artistic creation and making. He says:

[The artist's] work is not experiment but engagement – engagement which enlarges that which it employs by the risk of extending it beyond its known capacity. As the artist

2 Vanstone, *Love's Endeavour*, p. 46.
3 Arguably the greatest novel of them all.
4 Vanstone, *Love's Endeavour*, p. 46.

exceeds his known powers, his work is precariously poised between success and failure, between triumph and tragedy: it may be that the work of art is marred beyond redemption, or it may be that powers hitherto unknown will prove adequate to the completion and triumph of the work.[5]

Improvisation – engaging with the unforeseen – is neither a kind of undisciplined form of play nor a rule-bound experimental process. It may have moments of experimentation, but ultimately it is participatory engagement in risky relationship. It entails a faithful but risky relationship between creator and created thing; between artist and art.

I am most acutely aware of attempting to live this faithful, risky relationship in my efforts to be a poet. As a poet, I'm conscious of the ways in which I want to test the edges and boundaries of technique and form and, crucially, what may be said or not said. The poem is no mere object in my hands; it speaks back, and, most excitingly of all, 'surprises' me, certainly if it's a decent poem. If I set out – as I sometimes have – with a presumption about the shape and possibility of a poem it is mostly a recipe for failure. For I will attempt to exercise too much control over the artefact, the poem. In short, there is a precariousness in the poet's discipline and craft, as in all artistic craft. Most of my writing fails, and certainly if I am to write anything of value it requires the risk of failure. Rehearsing that which has succeeded previously simply won't make poetry. Poetry disrupts the maker as much as any member of its audience. It can change us in its precarious openness. Vanstone captures something when he says of the art-maker, 'Each decisive step is a precarious step, to be redeemed from tragedy only by the next and equally precarious step, of correction or new discovery, which must be improvised to succeed it.'[6]

Here one comes to the rub: the precariousness of Christ's redeeming work. When one thinks carefully about it, one can only be struck by how absurd and fraught and strange the

---

5 Vanstone, *Love's Endeavour*, p. 47.
6 Vanstone, *Love's Endeavour*, p. 48.

whole matter is. For whatever else it might be, the story of Jesus is a story of a seeming nobody, a king without a crown made of anything other than thorns, a lord whose seat of authority is either a manger or a cross. Born of peasants or near-peasants in a genuinely no-note province of what was then the greatest empire on earth, Jesus' impact in his lifetime barely extended beyond 100 miles and then primarily among fisherfolk, the once-possessed, the half-healed and the insignificant. He was not a child of privilege or salon or the academy. He was born in obscurity and died a criminal's death. If we proclaim him Messiah, Lord, King and Son of God, we do so through his unobtrusive and mostly ignored redeeming work, which nonetheless unpicks every tangled and damaged thread of the universe and rethreads it with love and reconciliation. This is the One who reveals his reconciliation first to women and makes himself known in the breaking of bread. He greets his friends on the shore and breaks the flakes of the sea with them over a bonfire.

I have not said anything new or radical or even terribly fresh. Nonetheless, for some the very strangeness and ridiculousness of this picture of Love's redeeming work will be sufficient to discount it as fantasy and fairy tale. I do understand this. I have been there. For many years I stood among the mockers and the sceptics and – these comprise the majority now, I think – the indifferent. However, what if one dares to take this story as revealing the economy of the kingdom of love? Surely, it can only speak of a God who dares precariousness; no, more than that, who has to dare precariousness for the work of redemption and reconciliation to be of any use and transformation. For surely, if there was another way, God would take it. He would not go along with such an absurd scheme if it were not necessary.

Herein lies what, for me, is at the centre, the axis, of God's necessary precariousness and vulnerability. When Christ says, 'Thou shalt love the Lord thy God with all thy heart, and with all thy soul, and with all thy strength, and with all thy mind; and thy neighbour as thyself', one probably hears it as rule and imperative. It can sound merely legal. I think we are called to hear it first and foremost as invitation and reminder. It is a call back to the truth of relationship. It is simply that we find ourselves being our completest selves when we live in God and in each other and in peace with ourselves. But this is not some abstract work, but the work of the living across time and space with all its mess and fragility. It is indwelling. If it is to be love, as we have seen, it cannot be coercive or forced. It has to have openness, the possibility of tragedy and the stature of waiting.

The stature of waiting. Again, Vanstone is helpful. He says, 'The precariousness of love is experienced, subjectively, in the tense passivity of "waiting". For the completion of its endeavour, for its outcome as triumph or as tragedy, love must wait.'[7] Love's redeeming work, according to this picture, is characterized by the willingness to wait – quietly, unobtrusively and perhaps even silently, without expectation – for a response that may not come, for a reciprocity that may not be available.

We may wait and never receive love in return or even be noticed. It entails allowing the other to be free to be themselves and walk away. Waiting, on this picture, is a token of letting go, of refusing the temptation to seek control or be bumptious. In offering love, one trusts that that which is freely offered might as easily be refused. One might become that fool, that schmuck who waits and never receives even a glance. I sense this is where the notion of 'truth' finds its real charge and weight. For in being invited to live in and on the truth of God's love, the conception of 'truth' being offered is not that which might be conceived as 'doctrine' or 'dogma' but a betrothed relationship. Troth and truth are, here, basically the same, meaning intimacy – full, trusting relationship. This is not the realm of right belief or even right practice. It is right relationship, and right relationship has the character of gift.

God in Jesus Christ offers a love that has the form of gift – of self-giving, of a life for others – and because it is gift it does not demand or require reciprocity. However, one may discover – as I and countless others have – that in acknowledging and receiving the gift, one wants to make a response.

---

7 Vanstone, *Love's Endeavour*, p. 49.

Indeed, in Christ's self-giving he reveals the likeness into which we are called. He shows the structure of truthful personhood. If by person – drawing on the Latin, *per* meaning 'through' and *sonare* meaning 'to sound' – one might claim that a person is a 'through-sound' or 'that which is sounding through ...' On this picture, Christ reveals that the fullness of our personhood is shown when we 'sound through' with Love. I think it's that simple, and that elusive. It's that absurd and marvellous: we are called to sing and be sung by Love. That's a life worthy of God, and a life we so often clumsily stumble towards.

I'm sure some who have stuck with this chapter will be frustrated that I have not sought to define Love. It is tempting to offer structural analyses based on things like Lewis's *Four Loves*. To talk of *agape*, *storge*, *philia* or *eros* can give shape, though it can also create the illusion of discrete compartments for Love's work. We can create taxonomies in which certain 'kinds' or 'types' of love are privileged over others. I understand why one might want to prioritize *agape* over other accounts of love. However, if God reveals the priority of *agape* in Love's saving work, surely that matters little without desire and friendship and intellectual care and sympathy.

So, I want to be discreet about definitions. Definitions always exclude. Perhaps, like Wittgenstein, it is better to speak of family resemblance. I want to acknowledge that God – as artist and lover – finds his work of creating and making, his work of love and redemption, caught up in the gap between triumph and tragedy. He offers himself to a fragile, half-healed, much-traumatized world and invites us to participate in the relationship that sets us free to grow into his likeness. His love is authentic, and therefore he allows us to walk away from that invitation. That permission is a token of love, of his love for us. It is the price, delight and cost of authentic love and its tender possibilities. It is a love maintained in the knowledge that there will be some who will not be able to receive or even recognize the fact of resurrection demonstrated in the Garden on Easter Day. It is a love offered to those of us who seem unable to get beyond the seeming and actual tragedy of Good Friday or living through the absences of Holy Saturday. It is love offered in the midst of trauma which may overwhelm us or drive us. It is love which knows that any one of us might join the ranks of the shattered and overwhelmed. Equally, it is love maintained among those who, for whatever reason, fetishize the cross. That is, those who look at the cross and make of its tragic performance of 'Love destroyed' too obvious or too quick a triumph or victory. It is a love maintained when any of us, with our multiform sureties and clumsy certitudes, end up putting our fingers through the delicate web of love God weaves.

However, for all our clumsiness and bumptious religiosity, for all our wounds and trauma and bewilderment, still the Garden of Resurrection waits. It waits because for all Love's precariousness, paradoxically, it has a power that surpasses any other: within it lies the universe's Divine Comedy, its tender, unassuming victory. Within it lies the absurd possibility of resurrection, which comes towards us in the one who – because we spurned his gift of love and crushed it on a cross – might reasonably be expected to seek revenge. But he does not. Rather he responds to the surprise and strangeness of resurrection with an offer: of reconciliation and richer relationship and, well, a chance to begin again in mutual love and a willingness to be in the hands of each other. And if there is solidarity in our traumas to be found in the cross, it is not enough. Not for transformation. And if Shelly Rambo is right that dwelling on Holy Saturday may offer us space to find solidarity, it is not enough.[8] However, if the site of our traumas and our dreams and our longings is to be remade as a site of promise and gift, the witness of the Garden is the beginning of new community and indwelling.

God desires to meet us in the Garden and in the Upper Room and on that road that leads away from Jerusalem to Emmaus. He invites us to place our questioning, doubting hands in his

8 Shelly Rambo, *Spirit and Trauma: A Theology of Remaining* (Louisville, KY: Westminster John Knox Press, 2010). See, also, Shelly Rambo, *Resurrecting Trauma: Living in the Afterlife of Trauma* (Waco, TX: Baylor University Press, 2017), and Karen O'Donnell, *Broken Bodies: The Eucharist, Mary and the Body in Trauma Theology* (London: SCM Press, 2019).

wounds and side. He comes alongside us on the lonely road as we head away from the catastrophe of loss; he comes alongside us as we process the bizarre rumours of resurrection and reconciliation emerging from Easter Day and our own bewildering Jerusalems. He comes alongside us as we head away down towards Emmaus, on that path we feel we must walk, in our bewilderment and hope and fear.

Christ comes alongside us and, in the evening of the day, turns the rumour of Love into its fulfilment in the breaking of bread. He who is the completeness of Love becomes our companion and we his. We imagine that we offer him hospitality, but it is he who offers it to us. For as the Old French *compaignon* has it – drawing on the Latin *com*, meaning together, and *panis*, meaning bread – true companionship is found in the breaking of bread. Relationship. Love. Precarious hope. Sometimes, just sometimes, it's that simple and it's that strange. Perdition is turned into promise in simple works of precarious love, in broken bread and in wine outpoured. It will not sort everything, or keep us safe from a world at risk of falling apart. It will offer sustenance for the next step of the journey, and it will ensure we remember that we are not expected to walk it alone.

6

God in the Company of the Kindly Ones

In Euripides' *Bacchae*, Tiresias – the blind prophet – says, 'To the gods we mortals are all ignorant.' It is a moment of ironic clarity which Pentheus, King of Thebes, fails to recognize. Pentheus, representative and preserver of law and order, military hard man and patriarch, cannot see what the blind prophet sees. He thinks he is a match for his opponent and cousin, Dionysus, the god of wine, communal ecstasy and dancing. Pentheus – who operates through what we might call the cynical clarity of *real politik*, in which the capacity to control power via law and civil authority determines reality – cannot grasp his own ignorance in the face of the Divine. He refuses to treat properly with his fragility and precariousness.

Pentheus' antagonist Dionysus returns to Thebes as the Stranger with his band of female worshippers, the Maenads, to take vengeance on Pentheus for disallowing worship of him, this new god from the East. For Pentheus refuses to acknowledge that Dionysus is a son of Zeus. Again and again, Pentheus fails to spot the cunningly disguised Dionysus' traps that will ultimately lead to his destruction at the hands of the Maenads or Bacchae. Through a series of ploys, Dionysus draws the over-controlled and controlling Pentheus into a scheme that will spell his doom.

When Pentheus resolves to kill the (from his perspective) out-of-control Maenads, Dionysus appeals to Pentheus' voyeurism, persuading him to observe the women before acting. It leads Pentheus – by now half-crazed and ecstatic himself and ever more under the spell of Dionysus – to his doom at the hands of the frenzied Maenads. The Maenads include Pentheus' own mother, Agave, and his aunts. Believing Pentheus to be a lion, Agave tears off Pentheus' head and takes it on a stick to Cadmus, his grandfather and the founder of Thebes. In the post-ecstatic reality, of course, Agave comes to realize the terrible sin she has committed against her son, and the house of Cadmus is broken in the face of the god Dionysus. In Mike Poulton's striking 2010 version of the *Bacchae*, Agave says, at the play's conclusion, 'Where am I to go?/ The earth will find no rest/for my god-cursed weight', to which Cadmus replies, 'My heart no longer beats –/ I have no wounding words of love/ nor anything to give you.' Agave is banished.[1]

It is the Chorus, of course, who supply the final gloss on the *Bacchae*'s catastrophic staging of an encounter between human pride and the surety of the gods. In Poulton's version, the Chorus sing:

> The gods look down upon our hopes and fears
> and watch, unseen, our journey through the world
> shattering our certainties, or answering our prayers,
> accomplishing, or leaving unfulfilled
> the flattering visions of our destiny.

In the *Bacchae*, Dionysus plans his bloody vengeance and Pentheus cannot see that, in the hands of gods, men are play-things, subject to the gods' power. Humans are, by turns, to be used by the gods or have their prayers answered. Pentheus' inability to read the facts of his violent world and his limited place in it will be his doom. Millennia later, Gloucester in *King Lear* captures the precariousness of a human in a world of gods when he says, 'As flies to wanton boys are we to the gods. They kill us for their sport.'

What kind of God is adequate to precariousness? I suspect answers to that question partly depend on one's starting point. While I am a committed Christian, I am someone who has also

---

1 Euripides, *The Bacchae*, adapted by Mike Poulton (London: Oberon Books, 2010). Poulton renders Agave as Agaue.

been nourished by ancient Greek ideas of the divine and when I consider this gift it affects my answer. For I was formed, as an undergraduate and postgraduate philosophy student, in Greek conceptions of justice, subjectivity and so on. I became familiar with concepts of Form and Truth, Virtue and Beauty. I remember, as a callow sixth former, being greatly impressed by Alfred North Whitehead's claim that 'The safest general characterization of the European philosophical tradition is that it consists of a series of footnotes to Plato.' For a while, the only philosopher I thought worthy of substantive addition was Aristotle. I guess I was a bit of a pillock. Teachers, tutors and friends also introduced me to the Greek gods and I greeted them in all their capriciousness, weirdness and delight; through Homer, Euripides, Aeschylus and so on, I've enjoyed (and been disturbed by) the company of Apollo, Dionysus and Artemis.

Donna Tartt's *The Secret History*, which focuses on a group of young people obsessed with the Classics, came out in the early stages of my postgraduate studies. I was *that* person who thought the book's dodgy characters were kind of cool, even though they are basically dreadful. Through the prism of Nietzsche and the postmoderns, I had become fascinated by the Greeks, and Tartt's cast of over-privileged characters were also fascinated by the Greeks. Perhaps it is unsurprising that I – a rather insecure student with a febrile imagination – childishly over-identified with Henry, Camilla, Charles and co. If I have moved on, and indeed come to carefully interrogate the mystique of Hellenic modes, the Greeks – philosophers, poets, dramatists and myth-makers – retain an enduring fascination. How they negotiate fragility and divinity present one line of investigation into the place of god/s in a world of precarity.

As I write this, I am self-isolating with symptoms of Covid-19, in the midst of the 2020 coronavirus pandemic. I am fortunate that I have good friends and a church family to support me. Nonetheless, the world feels a little more precarious than it did a few months ago. Still, it is simply the case that most people living in a privileged society like early twenty-first-century Britain do not live with the levels of precariousness experienced by Bronze Age people such as the ancient Greeks or the Hebrew people of King David's and Solomon's time. People living in the kingdoms of Judah and Israel or the Athenian Democracy didn't have access to the welfare, technological or medical resources we do today. For all I know, that time might have been Arcadia or a Very-Eden, but I doubt it. Life expectancy was short and the lines between flourishing and famine would have been narrow. The biblical accounts of famine and war, as much as Homer's account of the war on Troy, indicate the depth of precariousness that might beset the people living in that world.

I am not a classicist and so I offer my comments about precariousness and the Greeks tentatively and cautiously. Acknowledging that, however, there are themes in Greek mythology which, for me, indicate the extent to which their conceptions of the Divine represent a series of responses to precariousness. In short, I sense that embedded in the messy pantheon of Greek gods – who are represented as, by turns, capricious, selfish, vengeful and mean, as well as munificent, beautiful and magnificent – is a response to the question, 'Why is the world as it is?'

In suggesting that Greek myths offer a response to that question, I don't wish to suggest that the gods simply represent 'reverse-engineered' explanations for suffering or precariousness. It is not that they were merely invented as ways of giving an account of the miseries or limitations of a Bronze Age existence. That would be hardly worthy of intellectual assent; the nexus of human imagination is simply too rich for such a modernist, reductionist account. Human beliefs emerge out of contexts and conditions where people faced lives that might have glimpses of glory, but also a fair amount of pain, tragedy and arbitrariness. Reductionism will not do.

However, there are reasons the Greek gods and myths still speak. They know our precariousness and fragility and treat with them through one set of visions of the Divine. Thus, the Greek gods are typically represented as the wellspring of humanity's struggles. In his noted hymn to Zeus – chief among the gods – in the *Agamemnon*, Aeschylus writes:

Zeus, whatever he may be,
if that is the name he wishes to hear,
that is the name I shall invoke ...
to what may he be compared?
For – in the balance of all things –
only Zeus! Only he, if I am to cast off
the fruitless burden of care before I die.

Not even the one who was great of old,
raging with wild strength,
will be worthy of memorial,
and as for he who comes after,
he was thrice thrown down and is gone;
but he who sings to Zeus
will strike the very soul of wisdom.

Zeus! He is the guide to understanding,
he insists wisdom is found only in suffering;
still, in sleep my heart's wounds
seep with grief's memory,
until wisdom comes against my will.
It is the gift of the gods, who are majestic
at the helm, a violent grace.[2]

This is a heavily abstracted version of Zeus – 'Zeus, whatever
he may be,/ if that is the name he wishes to hear' – who nonetheless is marked down as the one 'who has given the command
"Learn by suffering"'. This is no comforting or comfortable
picture of the King of the Olympian gods. This is a testing and
trying god – seated in majesty – offering uncomfortable (and
indeed ambiguous) gifts.

The famous story of Pandora offers perhaps the most curious
account of the problematic and questionable gifts of the gods.

---

2 This is my own relaxed translation of Agamemnon's 'Hymn to
Zeus'. I know classicists will quail at my kindly interpretation of terms,
and the use of modern idiom. I want to convey the spirit of the speech,
laying particular emphasis on the notion that wisdom may be discovered via suffering (the *pathei mathos*).

Pandora – whose name is sometimes translated 'All-Gifted', 'All-Endowed', and sometimes 'All-Giving' – is in Greek tradition the first woman, created by Hephaestus by the command of Zeus. In Hesiod's account, each god co-operated to give her individual gifts and she was – ultimately – a wonder for both gods and men. Pandora – in one version of the story – is offered as a gift by Zeus to the Titan Epimetheus. Epimetheus' (famous) brother Prometheus – who made humanity from clay and stole fire from the gods – warns his sibling against accepting gifts from Zeus, who Prometheus rightly suspects plans revenge for Prometheus' theft. Epimetheus, alas, is not as fleet-witted as his brother and accepts Pandora as a gift from Zeus. She arrives holding a jar she has been told never to open. The couple marry, have a daughter, and eventually curiosity gets the better of Pandora. She opens the jar and releases all manner of ills. When in her panic she recloses it, only one thing clings to the lip of the jar: 'hope' – or, as some translations have it, 'anticipation' of both good and bad – remains. Zeus, by his plot, restores the division between gods and men.

Consider also the myth of Niobe, the daughter of Tantalus and the wife of King Amphion of Thebes. According to Homer's *Iliad*, she had six sons and six daughters and boasted of her progenitive superiority to the Titan Leto, who had only two children, the twin deities Apollo and Artemis. Her boasting infuriates the gods and, as punishment for her pride, Apollo kills all Niobe's sons, and Artemis kills all her daughters. The bodies of the dead children lay for nine days unburied because Zeus had turned all the Thebans to stone, but on the tenth day they were buried by the gods. In one version of the myth, Niobe went back to her Phrygian home, where she was turned into a rock on Mount Sipylus (Yamanlar Dağı, northeast of Izmir, Turkey). This mountain continues to weep when the snow melts above it. In the *Metamorphoses*, Ovid says of Niobe, 'Look, Niobe comes … as beautiful as anger will let her be.'

If Niobe is the prototype of the bereaved mother, weeping angrily and desperately for the loss of her children, her story reiterates how readily, in the Greek myths, the gods punish human hubris and pride. It is simply the case that humans –

even humans who are heroes and demi-gods – need to know their place. Consider Hercules/Heracles. His father was Zeus and his mother was Alcmene/Alcmena. Hercules was conceived when Zeus disguised himself as Alcmene's husband Amphitryon. Hercules suffers persecution throughout his life because of the jealousy and hatred of Zeus' wife Hera. She even tries to murder him, sending two snakes to kill him in the cradle. Hercules wakes and crushes the great serpents with his bare hands.

These examples indicate the extent to which the gods and powers and forces found in Greek mythology need to be appeased and obeyed by mere mortals. Sometimes even that isn't enough. One strategy might be that adopted in the face of the Eumenides. The Eumenides – 'the Kindly Ones' or 'the Gracious Ones' – is a name sometimes given to the Furies, the three goddesses of vengeance: Tisiphone (avenger of murder), Megaera (the jealous) and Alecto (constant anger). In Anthony Powell's magisterial *A Dance to the Music of Time* sequence, the narrator proffers a fascinating explanation for the Greeks' decision to change the names of these goddesses from the Furies to the Kindly Ones. When he hears his parents' chef Albert describe 'suffragettes' as 'Virgin Marys', he remembers:

> At lessons that morning – the subject classical mythology – Miss Orchard had spoken of the manner in which the Greeks, because they so greatly feared the Furies, had named them the Eumenides – the Kindly Ones – flattery intended to appease their terrible wrath ... they inflicted the vengeance of the gods by bringing in their train war, pestilence, dissention on earth; torturing too, by the stings of conscience. That characteristic alone, I could plainly see, made them sufficiently unwelcome guests. So feared were they, Miss Orchard said, that no man mentioned their names, nor fixed his eyes on their temples.[3]

3 Anthony Powell, *The Kindly Ones* (London: Heinemann, 1962), pp. 2–3.

Aeschylus' *The Eumenides*, the second play in the *Oresteia* sequence, can be read as a text on the emergence of proper judicial order in Athens. In doing so it perhaps indicates one strategy for 'drawing the poison' or the power of the vengeful Furies. The Furies have been relentlessly pursuing Orestes for killing his mother, Clytemnestra. In desperation, exhausted from the pursuit, Orestes pleads to the patron goddess of Athens, Athena and, hearing his cry, she arranges a trial for him by 12 of his peers supervised by himself on the Areopagus. Orestes becomes the first plaintiff in a jury trial. After the trial comes to an end, the votes are tied. Athena casts the deciding vote and determines that Orestes will not be killed. The Furies are – well – furious, but Athena eventually persuades them to accept the decision and, instead of violently retaliating against wrongdoers, become a constructive force of vigilance in Athens. She changes their names from the Furies to the Eumenides, the 'Gracious Ones'. Athena then ultimately rules that all trials must henceforth be settled in court rather than being carried out personally. The Furies – agents of vengeance and our primal urge for 'blood-honour' – have the poison of violence drawn into the realm of justice. They find a new identity as the 'Kindly Ones'.

How does this sit in the economy of the Living God, the God of Abraham, Isaac and Jacob, who empties himself into Christ? Well, for a moment, suppose I apply the approach I've used regarding Greek gods to the biblical God. In short, supposing one imagines the pictures we have of the biblical God as a set of responses to radical precariousness. In doing so, what does the God represented by Jesus Christ reveal? The Greek pantheon certainly offers accounts of the emergence of suffering, pain and precariousness in the world: Zeus, in Aeschylus' terms, commands suffering as a means to revealing truth;[4] the Pandora myth presents an account – a theodicy, if you will –

---

4 In *Dazzling Darkness*, I explore whether the idea found in Greek tragedy, that suffering can lead to wisdom – the *pathei mathos* – has much traction. See Rachel Mann, *Dazzling Darkness* (Glasgow: Wild Goose, 2012), pp. 20–2.

which indicates that suffering enters the world at the hands of a woman, as punishment for transgression; more broadly, we discover that humanity's trials and absurdities are the result of playfulness and selfishness and vanity of the gods. In essence, we are caught up in the games of the Immortals against which we have no defence, except perhaps appeasement or wit or cunning. This, arguably, offers – for an enchanted, spiritually charged world – an account of why being human is such a precarious and troublous matter.

As already indicated in a previous chapter, I guess one classic Christian answer to the 'origin' of precariousness in our world lies in traditional readings of the myth of Eden. Thus – as traditional readings have it – the depredations of sin enter the world through the actions of Eve and Adam. They are given everything, including 'free will', and an instruction not to eat from the Tree of the Knowledge of Good and Evil. Of course, Eve and Adam do so eat, egged on by a serpent, and Eden is lost. The mother and father of us all are lost in perdition and sin, and cast out into a precarious world beyond Eden, where men till the soil with hardship and women suffer pain in child-birth. In Eden, God had given them – the crown of his creation – all that they needed, but they spurned the gift, and fell. The bust-up-ness of the world – its fragility and precarity and limit – is not (in terms of efficient cause) God's fault, but that of the humans, egged on by the serpent.[5] God's dignity and goodness is preserved.

I have already indicated that feminist and critical pressure can be brought to bear on the notion of 'Eden' as a kind of analogue of heaven/the ultimate safe space. Arguably, Eden already had precariousness written into it – the simple presence of a tree that can 'screw everything up' is an indication of this. The fact that a serpent prowls there too suggests that Eden was not all we imagine it was cracked up to be. Equally, Jewish scholars – for whom the story of Eden was a story long before it was ever a story for Christians – bring different emphases

---

5 By 'efficient cause' I mean, following Aristotle, 'the primary source of the change or rest'.

to those that both Protestant and Catholic Christians have become inured. For example, Rabbinic and Talmudic scholarship would be disinclined to read the story of Eve and Adam as an estrangement that requires messianic redemption to be healed. The practice and study of Torah renews intimacy with God and leads to eternal life. The Mishnah, the first part of the Talmud, includes this claim: 'The Holy One (blessed be He) created the Evil Inclination; He created Torah as its antidote.'[6]

The classic Christian analysis of fall and redemption always runs the risk of turning God's story of salvation into theory. It can end up offering an intellectualized account of the Christian God's adequacy to a precarious world. For, one way it is possible to present the story of sin, fall and redemption runs as follows: In the beginning, God created the earth and it was good, but then we messed it all up. We fell, because of our choices, into sin – a great sin against God's infinite mercy and justice and goodness. Because we mucked up the world, there was no way we could put it right; indeed, God would have been perfectly within his rights to destroy humanity. But God's mercy got the better of his anger. He came up with a solution. For while his infinite mercy may have allowed him to let things rest, his infinite justice demanded that payment for sin be made. Only an infinite payment would do – something only God could offer. But here's the problem: it was humans who fell in the first place, so the payment had to come from the human side – otherwise it wouldn't be a real payment. So, God came up with this cunning plan: send his Son into the world as a man so he could pay the price. Since he was human, his Son could fulfil the human requirement; because he was God he could make an infinite payment. And that payment was made by the cross. The full and sufficient sacrifice. A blood sacrifice of the son covers the sins of those who choose to follow him.

I hope I've not simply set up a straw-man version of the sub-

---

6 The *Jewish Study Bible*, 2nd edn, ed. Adele Berlin and Marc Zvi Brettler (Oxford: Oxford University Press, 2014), is full of insightful help and essays on how Jewish scholarship treats the Tanakh/Old Testament rather differently from Christian scholars.

stitutionary-atonement account of redemption. I don't simply want to knock it down without acknowledging its power and the way it tempts part of me. It appeals to my intellectual and bloodthirsty side, and my love of theory. I can also feel its power at the level of the body. It appeals to that bit of me – is it primitive? Is it formed by a kind of nasty bleakness that wants spectacle? Is it a cultural accretion? – which hankers for violent transactions. It is that bit of me that I share with all those who long for revenge for violent acts committed against the vulnerable;[7] it is that bit of me that, for all my civilized urbanity, is secretly fascinated by our culture's history of burnings, *auto-da-fé*, executions and Inquisition.

However, I also sense that, ultimately, the substitutionary-atonement position is an idolatrous account of redemption. This warrants some unpacking. Idols are made for us; they are part of our need for things that function for us. They may look impressive, but they exist to make us safe, make us look better or reinforce our self-identities and value. They become foci for our best and sometimes our worst aspects. They exist to make the way we are, and the place in which we are set, 'liveable'. They provide a way to stage-manage the human and the divine. The substitutionary-atonement theory arguably keeps God and us at one step remove; it doesn't invite our deeper participation; it indicates how God does stuff for us and – in so far as it invites participation – it expects intellectual assent.

Certainly, this intellectual assent may have implications for behaviour, especially when allied to a fearful threat of spending eternity in torment or hell should one fail to behave as God requires. Yet, this God strikes me as managed and as controlled as the Baals and the Golden Calf of the Old Testament. For all the talk of 'infinite mercy' and 'infinite justice' this is a God whose redemptive action operates according to a rule. As such

---

7 I recently experienced this reaction when reading Christina Lamb's extraordinary *Our Bodies, Their Battlefield* (London: William Collins, 2020), an account of the violence committed against women and girls in war. I was so incensed by the violence committed by the likes of Boko Haram and Burma's military that I could, in that moment, have sanctioned the vilest works of revenge.

he works according to structural imperatives we impose. There is surely a sense in which this picture of God – stage-managed, trapped in intellectual categories and logic systems, simultaneously angry and gracious according to a rule – is less attractive than the puckish, distressing complexity of the Greek gods. It is certainly less fun and interesting.

Of course, the God who saves – the God of Abraham, Isaac and Jacob and the God of Jesus Christ – is a God who meets the world's precariousness in quite other ways; in *living* ways. This is a God who is caught up in the midst and who redeems from within the midst, in relationship. The God of the Bible – of the Tanakh as much as the Christian gospel – is the God of relationship. And this is the only God adequate to our precariousness, our fragility. This is the God who meets our gift for perdition and failure, who meets this world's gift for precariousness, as the God of gift. He is the one who makes a gift of himself and says that the only adequate response to precariousness is to be in and be made in relationship.

Perhaps you are surprised that I use the phrase 'our gift for perdition and failure'. It may seem to give 'sin' too positive a feel. Perhaps I should talk about our 'propensity', 'disposition' or 'tendency', or even our 'dark talent' or 'genius', for wickedness. Gift is a risky word to use in the context of human behaviours that take in violence, misery and hate. I use it quite deliberately to invite us to 're-scope' our representation of ourselves and God in a world shaped by and for Gift. I don't want to suggest or imply that 'sin' is wonderful and delightful, in and of itself. I also absolutely want to distance myself from any claims for the delights of violence.

Rather, I want us to consider what we have to offer – 'What is our honest gift?' – in a world of precarity. This is another way of asking ourselves to treat with ourselves as honestly as we can. It may be a banal point, but it is worth restating: we hold within our species a talent for 'art' and 'making' and the possibilities of a longing for beauty and truth and goodness, but we are also always children of limit and compromise. We would be foolish, for example, to confuse a profound aesthetic sense for goodness. If I ever mistook 'beauty' for 'truth' I do not now. In Nancy Mitford's *Love in a Cold Climate*, Cedric may have an exquisite taste for beauteous *objets d'art*, but he is hardly an example of supreme human virtue.

In the presence of God, there is a liberating power in acknowledging what our gift is. When I say 'our gift' I want to be attentive to both the particular and the general implications. At the level of the particular, I know that I am a person of unclean hands and lips. I want to live and act for good, but I do not hold within me the resources to achieve it. Sure, I have not committed the grossest crimes, and I trust that I'm never likely to. In simple terms, I might claim that I am a 'good person'. However, I am compromised and limited, as we are all compromised. I may be made in the image of God, but to grow into the likeness of Christ often seems impossible. I am not good, and change seems a lifetime's work. However, the 'particular' and the 'personal' is insufficient to offer an account of our species' gift for getting it wrong. Clearly, the whole of creation is compromised, limited and precarious and our species' place within it more often has the character of an ecology of exploitation, greed and failure rather than an ecology of grace. That's us, in this limited world we occupy, and, in the midst of our serial failure to act for the good, what we have left as an offering is 'hope'.

Thus far, it may seem that I am merely commending the territory delineated by Pandora, without relying on the story's theodicy. However, my approach is as much about an invitation not to read our capacity for failure, foolishness and damage through the scope of 'shame'. By seeking to shift the discourse away from 'shame' to 'gift' I want to invite us to consider honestly who and what we are in a precarious world, while being the kind of creatures who can meet God's abundance with joy and delight; with the promise of real liberation.

This shift from 'shame' to 'gift' might seem of minimal significance, but I think not. If we accept – as I think we should – that the God-Who-Saves comes to us as abundant Gift, not holding back but emptying herself into the fragility of human being in Jesus Christ, the way in which we dare to greet her is significant. At one level, I'm not suggesting that the work of redemption is conditional on our attitude or disposition. I 'get' that God's work is God's work. Salvation is gift, regardless of our reception of it. Christ redeems. However, the shape, form and content of the gift is – ultimately – an invitation into full and joyous relationship with the Living God. And this *is* a living, embodied and dynamic matter, not an intellectual schema. It requires the whole of our embodiment, in all its queerness and particularity; in our disability and strangeness. How we – individually and communally – greet God's invitation embodies a potent way of modelling the gift of holiness in a wholly and holy precarious world.

Perhaps one of the reasons the Eucharist matters so much is that it is about encounter, feasting, the body and transformation. In faith, we meet and receive Christ. There is a deep physicality about the act and mystery of communion. And most of all it is an act of resistance against theorizing. Certainly, there are many theories of 'the meaning of the Eucharist', as well as debates about what 'happens' in the Eucharist, and there is a place for them. It is important that we reflect upon our faith. Doctrine matters. But the key moment in the Eucharist is a mysterious encounter that outruns the desire for understanding. It is an encounter with Gift.

In the drama of the Eucharist, confession is a necessary and key moment. It is part of our preparation to receive God into our guts. When I first came to faith, I would typically use the time of confession as a time of rather desperate searching around for sins to offer to God. I often found it a bleak section of the service. I'd scratch around for something worthy with which to bother the Divine. It was all a bit embarrassing. I began to relax when I recognized that this moment in the drama was not simply about me and my sin. Confession is both corporate and formal – in the best sense – and, actually, a great gift. For it is about community recognition and gesture. If it is formal, it is also real, because it is effective. In confession, the community of faith makes to God its gift: its honest acknowledgement of what we bring to the table of love. And there is great love in acknowledging, with clear sight, honesty and authenticity, that we are wrong. Indeed, there is joy. From joy may issue forth the truest response to the gift of God in a precarious world: thanksgiving.

In thanksgiving – in Eucharist – we receive God into our guts. The ancient Greek for 'feeling compassion' is *splagchnizomai*, which literally means 'being moved to one's bowels'. For in classical culture, the bowels were the seat of compassion and pity. We are children of compassion – of gut and of womb. We are children of thanksgiving who acknowledge our precarity and the precariousness of our world. And our hope lies in the God who makes himself precarious and says, 'My salvation lies in relationship, between you and me, and between each other. Come take my precariousness in bread and wine into your guts and be moved.' And we are sent out in love and service to the world, calling others into relationships of love, compassion and peace. We become the living guts of the world.

7

God in a World of Cruel Optimisms

In *Wartime*, his remarkable and original study of American and British behaviour and belief during World War Two, Paul Fussell notes how maintaining 'morale' became a key way in which to structure and negotiate precariousness. Crucially, in the depths of a war that dragged on and on, the concept of 'accentuating the positive' came to be treated as an imperative. This is understandable, perhaps. For, in the face of the traumatic facts of the front line, it is unsurprising that the typical GI's or Tommy's (or German's) letter ran, 'Don't worry, Mum, I'll be fine', rather than, 'Mother, I'm scared to death'. Even if they'd written the latter it would not have survived censorship. Morale – with all its implications of good conduct, confidence and optimism – had to be maintained, both among those on the front line and on the home front. As Fussell notes, 'those attentive to the maintenance of home-front morale became skilled at optimistic prose'.[1]

My remarks on fragility, on the compromised body and human hope might seem very far removed from the anxiety and often cruel precariousness generated by wartime conditions. That's true, of course. In a privileged country like the UK, war can feel very distant.[2] War is something that happens elsewhere. I sense, however, that there are more intersections between wartime conditions and our own than we might readily admit.

---

1 Paul Fussell, *Wartime* (Oxford: Oxford University Press, 1989), p. 146.
2 Though in the light of anxieties generated by the coronavirus pandemic, perhaps we have begun to understand a little more about the restrictions of 'wartime'.

If the threats we feel for our present and our futures – climate change, social and cultural decay into nativism and populism, viral threats, conditions where work doesn't pay – can seem diffuse compared to the immediacy of threatened death in an air raid or in battle, we encounter, as much as our wartime forebears, the fragility and power of language in the hands of sophisticated media, propaganda and advertising.

Indeed, we live in and through what philosophers like Charles Taylor call 'imaginaries' – social and cultural and personal networks of meaning. In that regard, I'm not sure that we are very much different from those who lived 80-odd years ago. As in World War Two, we live in a time where crisis is represented through, understood and facilitated via language, symbol and the sophisticated use of media and advertising. As much as those who lived through the violent upheavals of the nastiest war in history, we can ask: how do we use language, relationship and symbol to cope, shape and form ourselves? What are the fantasies and myths that make our versions of precariousness 'livable'? What is the iconography of hope that is available to us in times such as these?

Fussell reminds us that in a time of anxiety and precariousness – especially in contexts saturated by the 'trickeries' of advertising and a longing for 'escape' and 'fantasy' – language's ever-fraught capacity to speak truth comes under intense threat. He points out that, by World War Two, official 'euphemism' had reached new heights.[3] Making tragedy, fear and fragility 'livable' – 'seemly' even – became an indispensable tool of propagandized cultures and societies. Words were offered that simultaneously underlined the precariousness of war while offering coping strategies. Thus, a panicky retreat, as at the Kasserine Pass in 1943, was designated a 'retrograde movement'. Finishing off the enemy was often called 'mopping-up',

---

3 In his earlier study of the Great War, *The Great War and Modern Memory* (Oxford: Oxford University Press, 1975), Fussell already indicates how official language – especially in British contexts – had already achieved prophylactic effects.

which, as Fussell notes, suggests domestic rather than military activity. He also says:

> From General Montgomery's practice of designating a forth-coming battle a *party* to the RAF's calling a 4000-pound bomb a *cookie*, the British showed a marked talent for using subtle nomenclature to soothe fears. *Battledress* is an example. That term seems to redeem some of the horror of *battle* by associating it with the harmless charms of normal *dress*, as in 'Do we dress for dinner?' or 'Oh, what a lovely dress!'

These euphemisms made both war and its effects 'seemly', while underlining its beastliness. The skilled reader – both then and now – is alert to the ironic effects when we use language to soften: it draws further attention to the beastly and makes it taboo.[4]

As people who live in conditions of sophisticated advertising, social media and screwy party-political propaganda, I guess none of the above surprises us. We are used to language and image being used to generate feelings and trigger emotional responses rather than speak truth. We are used to living in a time where it is difficult to discern the difference between falsehood and fact. We are inured to a 'reality' in which 'presentation' trumps 'actuality'. Fussell traces the emergence of a culture shaped by 'misinformation' – or (at the very least) by what words and images can be forced to mean – to the interwar advances in advertising. In particular, to its capacity to exploit the emergent media of the day, not least the radio, cinema and – in its nascent form – television. He suggests that 'by the time of the Second [War], there was prepared for it a well-organised profession skilled at disingenuous presentation and adept at imposing value on the neutral or the nugatory'.[5]

---

4 See, for example, the euphemisms for death we currently use: pass, passing (as well as some from the war – 'gone for a burton'). By avoiding 'death' they underline it.

5 Fussell, *Wartime*, p. 154.

A gift for presentation over actuality, allied to an instinct for using word and image to nudge content and feeling, is not least of the advertiser's gifts. Not every advertiser is a Goebbels, of course, but Fussell suggests (writing in 1989), 'as the current popularity of periodicals like the *National Enquirer*, *Star*, and *Globe* suggests, the Goebbels world, or something like it, is one of the most noticeable legacies from the Second World War to the present'.[6] I wonder what Fussell might have made of the internet and, specifically, social media.

Where I think these conditions hit 'pay-dirt' for people like us, living in conditions where one's grasp on 'reality', 'truth', 'fact' can feel exceedingly precarious, is in our attempts to live the/a 'good life'. Most of us have no shortage of information. We do not live under wartime conditions where propaganda ministries control the flow of data. Rather, we are overwhelmed by information that may or may not be true, and we are so saturated in advertising and bias and spin that we are unsure by what criteria we might judge between true and false and fact and fiction.

Nonetheless, one can be left feeling that one is not quite flourishing. We sense that the 'good life' – a life lived in truth and hope and love and virtue – might just be possible! And, then, we stop ourselves and ask, 'But can one trust words like "truth" or "hope" or even "love" in a culture that has so thoroughly used them to sell things or fan our desire?' Equally, many of us are aware that the world in which we live is not flourishing quite as we might hope it would. We are alert to the facts of climate change or the shame of mass homelessness or the fact that, in a wealthy nation, usage of foodbanks goes up year-on-year. We know something is wrong and yet we can feel paralysed. We are constantly presented with 'counter-narratives'; we do not trust the information available via the web or via traditional media, or – more likely – we become bunkered and over-trust those articles or webpages that confirm our prejudices.

---

6 Fussell, *Wartime*, p. 154.

We see the world burn, and rivers burst their banks, and our friends frightened about pandemics, and yet we are bombarded with emails and messages and ads telling us that we should focus on other things. However, if we focused on putting out a world on fire, what are the things which we have or which we want that would have to be lost? Day after day I receive emails and messages and internet ads telling me I deserve that long-haul trip to some rare destination, or inviting me to get excited about the food trends of the coming year. My desire for gratification, allied to my sense that 'yes, I do deserve this treat or that', is fanned almost constantly.

I, as much as anyone, just want to live and I want to live well and kindly and be known as a good person. That's how most of us want to live. Sometimes, I just want to survive and get through this week or this day. Sometimes I am assaulted by visions of what the 'good life' might be – how it might entail having fewer attachments in this world or being fitter or more relational or not buying 'stuff'. Sometimes I go on the internet or look out of my window and I get scared for the future, because right now it can feel like there's so little promise in the world. We all want to feel it's all going to be okay; we amuse ourselves and distract ourselves in order to cope in a world we worry has no sustainable future. We want our children or our siblings' children to have a future that is good and healthy and *possible*, and we want to be good and healthy, but it's not clear how that can happen. For – given how limited the resources of this planet are – how can the stable, comfortable life be possible for all?

We close our eyes and disengage or we engage and become angry and shouty; we retreat and we panic and we dream and we look for visions of the good life and are unsure it is possible, or sometimes we give in to simplistic ideas of what that good life might be. We say, 'If only we didn't do this or do that; if only our country/nation/town/village wasn't this or that; if only those people weren't here it would be good and safe and kind. It would no longer be precarious.' And we can feel all these things in the space of an hour or a morning or a day.

I am convinced that we are the fictional species. What I mean is that we are the species that very obviously lives via myth and fantasy and projection; we use story to tell us – as communities and individuals – who we are. We are the 'imaginary' species. In Charles Taylor's sense, we have imaginaries that shape and form and construct us. And one mode of that fictional richness is our capacity to construct multivalent 'presentations' which make actuality 'livable'. This is not – I think – necessarily sinful. It just is. We are a species with a genius for representing ourselves through other media. We use books, visual culture and slogans to tell ourselves who we are or who we want to be. We can and do live through myth and story. Is this a symptom of our precariousness or our genius? Or both?

The cultural critic Lauren Berlant developed a concept, 'cruel optimism', as a kind of diagnostic device to comprehend the kind of late-capitalist, neo-liberal world many of us live in and through. For Berlant, this is a world characterized by intense information, of insatiable appetite and (for the countries of the economic North) relative comfort, alongside a growing economic/social and political insecurity and precariousness. Berlant suggests, 'a relation of cruel optimism exists when something you desire is actually an obstacle to your flourishing'.[7]

For Berlant, 'optimism' is the 'force that moves you out of yourself and into the world in order to bring closer the satisfying *something* that you cannot generate on your own, but sense in the wake of a person, a way of life, an object, project, concept, or scene'.[8] It might involve food or love or a political project or some idea of the good life. For example, it might take the form of a new diet which promises to transform one's relationship with one's own body, or a political party which offers a way of making the world a better place. It might, I think, include 'catching' a vision of something in a book, and not just the motivational variety. As children of the fictive, we might attempt to live through the 'magic' of Harry Potter, or want to shape ourselves in terms of fictional role models from

---

7 Lauren Berlant, *Cruel Optimism* (Durham, NC: Duke University Press, 2011), p. 1.

8 Berlant, *Cruel Optimism*, pp. 1–2.

Lizzie Bennet through to Lord Peter Wimsey.[9] Berlant says, 'these kinds of optimistic relation are not inherently cruel. They become cruel only when the object that draws your attachment actively impedes the aim that brought you to it initially.'[10]

In essence, Berlant invites us to stop being 'sentimental' about the precarity and queerness of being bodies thrown into a bewildering world. Our optimistic fantasies about living a good life are just that. We may attempt to take hold of visions of the good life – whether that be conventional ones produced by historical modes of society like 'romance' or heteronormative conceptions of marriage or, alternatively, ones determined by visions that are a little more outré – but we are ultimately condemned to trauma and tragedy.

Let's see if I can unpack this in a rather less abstract manner. As subjects living in a time of profound individualism, constructed and shaped by a potent visual and literary culture (sophisticated and targeted advertising, brilliantly immersive TV and film etc.), one might be tempted to read one's life as a kind of story or a film. Indeed, there have been occasions when I've found it almost impossible not to do so. I don't think this is because I'm especially egotistical. Rather, it's just part of the cultural milieu in which we live. One might read oneself and one's close relations as the centre of a drama – as having a story arc. Life, on this view, has shape and, potentially, purpose. With sufficient skill and focus and 'vim' and 'talent' and a bit of luck, we might even imagine we can be the author of our own story. Rather like David Copperfield, in the new film adaptation by Armando Iannucci, one might find oneself writing and performing the book of one's own life.

However, we also live with a sense – an instinct, a feeling (often an educated one, grounded in harsh experience) – that skill or hard work or talent isn't enough. Precariousness leaks out of the world and out of our bodies and disrupts our optimisms – our strategies of success. We cannot guarantee

---

9 Or, if one were an atheist, one might add Christ to that list of fictional role models.

10 Berlant, *Cruel Optimism*, p. 1.

our happy ending. Life is not a comedy. And yet we continue to strive. We sense our happy ending is just out of reach; and often we settle for less and call it our happy ending, our 'good life'.

In Berlant's original US context, perhaps the acme of a cruel optimism is the American Dream. This is the national story that says that anyone can go from rags to riches; that anyone, with sufficient vim, can achieve. One might offer, at a seemingly lower level, the common experience of finding one's emotional and psychological sense of well-being being caught up in the success or failure of a sports team. 'Maybe next year' is the classic refrain of the disappointed football fan; great store can be placed on faithfulness to an authentic 'local' team that lacks the means to buy success. Yet, many become fans of successful teams – they want to be attached to success. How many people became Newcastle or Liverpool or City or United fans in the midst of their pomp?

The brilliance of Berlant's approach, even if one has questions about it, is how she delineates – like many 'affect theorists' – how we experience and feel things before we intellectualize them. We are already caught up in nexuses and scenes that provide 'stages' or 'platforms' for our bodies to emotionally engage and be formed. She offers a diagnosis of the present that has genuine power. How many of us have not experienced the feeling that 'x' is to be resisted or may be empty, but felt the voice – ours or another's – whispering, 'Oh, go on, you deserve a treat'? She understands mood and atmosphere and how they go ahead of us, and indicates why many of us – me included – can engage in barely rational activities like 'hoarding' or 'overeating'. She understands how we might rationalize our drives to own, possess and acquire far beyond any necessity, or seek after stratagems to extend our lives or consciousness. As 'affective' creatures we are also always at risk of tipping over into 'disaffection'; those things that offer us optimistic ways of going on – going to the gym, being on a diet, spending time in prayer and with family – may readily become the trigger for disaffection.

Perhaps one of the cruellest optimisms is generated by the

impact of escapist storytelling on those who might already be othered, marginal or queer. Consider the impact of a global sensation like the Harry Potter series. It offers a particularly imaginative opportunity for escapism. While almost all humans have a joy in escapist and fantastical concepts and literation, perhaps its greatest power is going to be for those who – through their sense of being different or marginal – most especially need or want escape. Harry Potter provides a ready-made universe through which marginal humans may read themselves and with whom they may identify. However, one of the factors – not always immediately obvious, especially to younger minds – that makes this series so ubiquitous and popular is its conventionality: it takes place in a traditionally binaried world, in which girls brew 'love potions' and boys are grumpy gits and are a bit lazy.

Harry Potter comments on our world by being very like it. However, it is just queer enough for a wide range of people to escape into it. The conventionality and its desire to be 'normal' make this series so potently effective in our culture. This is a recipe for disappointment for queer people: for its conventionality ensures that they are introduced to it; its fantasy means that they have means to escape into it, only to find later that their liberation is constrained by it. They discover that its author is not as amazing as they thought – indeed is perhaps conventional and disappointing; they find that the thing that has offered liberation or grounds for optimism is cruel.

Berlant is attentive to the way in which wider political movements from Occupy on the Left to the most right-wing Nationalist group emerge out of affective moments: Occupy might be read as a response to the cruel optimism of capitalism, which sells a dream of fulfilment through money that it can't deliver; the populism of Trump or Bolsanaro is a response to the cruel optimisms of the flourishing society where none are left behind. She offers an account of the human genius for encountering the world as affective, problematic and problematized bodies. She 'gets' our gift for traumatizing ourselves and others. She gets that our ways of going on – seemingly full of hope and promise and goodness – are fantastical and will let us down.

It is not that Berlant and those who work in affect theory are suggesting that affect, emotion and experience are bad. That's not the point. The power of the approach is to indicate that when any of us claim that we are 'super-rational' or our arguments are definitive because of their logic or grounding in x, y or z, there will be nexuses and patterns and scenes of commitment that are already in play. Sometimes we can deploy argumentative and critical approaches that are presented as better than 'mere emotion', which we tag 'rational' or 'reasonable'; we can talk of facts and truth, and make strong cases for them. However, Berlant effectively suggests that we should pay attention to the back-stories and discursive strategies that some ways of carving-up the world rely on. For example, sometimes trans people are told that they are delusional; that their claims are fake or false or impossible. Sometimes those who deploy those arguments rely on 'natural law', 'revealed'/religious law or particular readings of science. Most of those arguments will appeal to reason or rationality or scientific fact and parody trans people as 'fantasists' or 'damaged'. Berlant wants to remind us that – for all their claims to objectivity, indisputable power and so on – those things that present themselves as the embodiment of the objective or rational will have affective histories, stories and commitments which partly determine how they read the world.

In theological terms, I suspect – if it were possible to tempt her – Berlant would suggest that rather than 'humans' being Eden's cast-offs, we were never made for Eden in the first place. Eden is perhaps the acme of our visions of 'cruel optimism': it is the dream of perfection and the good life, which is fundamentally unlivable without horizons of cruelty. The more we seek Eden, the more we fail to achieve it. Indeed, it may be the shadow that lurks in all of our present visions of the good life, just as some might argue that the strange times we live in – with their shouty politics, divisive and very public emotionalism, and the obsession with happy endings – are moments in late and decaying Christianity.

If Berlant's affective analysis of cruel optimism really does capture something about the way humans currently live, where does that leave those of us committed to Christianity? In one sense, it rather evens out the playing field. Affective theory reminds us that we are not, first, intellectual entities making our commitments on the basis of cool rationality, but already living bodies negotiating fantasy, myth, cultural ideas of goodness and our unavoidable sense of precariousness. We latch on to words and ideas and images and they latch on to us and we try to find ways to cope. Christian stories of sin and fall and redemption might – according to this picture – lose their transcendent power, but they can still exercise potent affective power. They present an account – however feebly or oddly – of what it means to live as bodies thrown into the world. The question is: is this schema 'cruel'? Does the desire to be formed into the likeness of Christ pull us painfully and tragically out of shape?

Perhaps it does. Indeed, perhaps it is the ultimate cruel optimism. The religious schema in its various forms is typically based on human inadequacy and God's adequacy. That is, we need to change to be more like him so that we can be saved, improved, transformed and so on. For countries like the UK or the USA, which live in the shadow or the echo of Christianity and Christendom, Christ's perfection becomes the regulatory icon for perfection, goodness and wholeness. Robert Graves claimed that the last thing a Christian loses when he loses his faith is the idea of Christ as the ideal man; perhaps the last thing that a Christian society loses when it abandons Christianity is the Christian life as its ideal.

And yet … it's tempting to respond to Berlant's schema by pointing out that a faith like Christianity is grounded in 'hope' rather than 'optimism'. Is that a cheap move? Berlant would be inclined to parse both categories, I suspect; she would wish to indicate that the language of hope presents a sophisticated sublimation or powerful translation of what might better be called optimism. In this regard, it is worth rehearsing Berlant's definition of 'optimism': it is the 'force that moves you out of yourself and into the world in order to bring closer the satisfying *something* that you cannot generate on your own'. On these terms, perhaps the religious mode represents a defining, if not the defining, example of optimism as a cultural category.

Nonetheless, if optimism is to be construed as an affective category, hope is surely a promissory one. It is, in short, about living on promises. I think there is power in this picture. What it can offer, at its best, is a critique of – for example – optimism projects like the American Dream. In Berlant's terms, the great attraction of the Dream is to fuse one's private fortune with that of the nation. It provides a 'global' landscape on to which one can project one's small desires for achievement and happiness: through it, one's story becomes part of the Big Story. Furthermore, it relies on the concept that success could happen to anyone because – beneath the differences, deprivations, disadvantages and particularities of our bodies – we are all the same. What matters is how we overcome disadvantages or are inspired by others' examples to achieve something. In this respect, a vision like the American Dream is sentimental: it relies not only on a picture of finding ourselves in something greater, but that *any* plucky person can come to represent success or the national spirit and *move* others to become something. It is a motivational film plot written large.[11]

There are modes of Christianity – Christianities, if you will – that are sentimentalized optimisms, and indeed intersect with versions of the American Dream. These are kinds of 'cargo-cult' or even 'prosperity gospel' Christianities, in which relationship between adherent, tradition and God is essentially transactional: 'If I offer you "x", I will get "y"; if I offer you my life, my soul, my tithe and my holy commitment, then I shall be blessed with long life and happiness.' There are horizons of all traditions in Christianity that risk or even rely on this transactional model; certainly, no tradition of Christianity can claim immunity from transactional pressures in which an

---

11 See, for example, the 2009 movie *The Blind Side*, starring Sandra Bullock, Quinton Areon and Tim McGraw, which tells the 'true story' of Michael Oher, the African-American gridiron player's journey from homeless teen to one of the top players in the NFL. Despite its cheesiness and tendency to concentrate on a 'white saviour' story, I find it moving, inspiring and touching.

adherent might come to believe that if they only pray harder, or stick to a narrow and demanding devotional path, they will be blessed mightily and receive all good things.[12]

This is unsurprising. There is a dimension of faith that invites adherents and potential adherents to unite their small story to the Big Story of God. And I would not want to deny the affective dimensions of our faith. That's what's helpful about the levelling Lauren Berlant brings about: she invites all of us, whether of faith or not, to be attentive to the affective. When I think about my own conversion to Christianity, there were intellectual and rational factors in play. Intellectually, as a one-time philosophy scholar, I sought to find my way through the paradoxes at the heart of Christianity. I toyed and reasoned, but I recognize that there was a much wider background wrestling that was not 'intellectual' or 'to do with argument'. It was to do with mood and atmosphere. I felt drawn towards God. Ultimately, I gave myself to God. In the words of Rossetti's famous poem, 'A Christmas Carol', 'What can I give him? … Give my heart.' My conversion was ultimately a heart matter. An educated heart, but a heart nonetheless.

I don't think my experience of faith is based on 'optimism', but 'hope'. Hope is a work of exposure and 'letting go'. It is about placing one's trust in an other who reveals themselves to be Gift and Life and Being of the world. What makes this work of hope and trust exhilarating and truth-full is that the letting go is not into the promise of success or achievement or self-actualization or even into goodness and loveliness. If Christ is the focus of faith, the growing into his likeness is an invitation

---

12 There will be some who would suggest that the currently fashionable mode in the Church of England operates out of a 'cargo-cult' mentality. For an account of this, see Andrew Brown and Linda Woodhead, *That Was the Church that Was* (London: Bloomsbury, 2017). Certainly, one can sometimes see in the C of E programmes an over-reliance on success models which say, 'That looks successful – popular, discipleship-nurturing – over there, let's try it here, here and here.' It is yet to be seen whether this will become a mode of cruel optimism in which what promises much for the church/the C of E becomes precisely the thing that will limit and damage it.

into failure and stripping away. It is about the way of death being the way of life. It is not about achievement. It is not sentimental. That's the promissory nature of hope – it is not the promise of pleasure or even the good life but the promise of progressive exposure to God's reality. And it is love – not as a romantic or sentimental or instrumental category – but God's solidarity and God's invitation into ways of resistance.

What I think it comes down to is the joy of not having to achieve, or be anything, or be more than the catastrophe and mess and unvirtuous person one actually is. The only level of wisdom required is to know that one is unwise and foolish and cannot achieve the completeness of the complete person – the good person or the holy person. For there is only one who is good and one who is holy. There is only one human being and it's OK to be more or less approximate.

As with optimism, 'hope' has precariousness inscribed in it. That is, if it is promissory, then promises are only as good as the one who makes the promise. When we attempt to live on promises made by a human or an institution we risk being let down; sometimes, I know only too well as a Christian that it can feel as if God lets us down in his promises to us, as a community or as persons. However, God is good and these promises are, ultimately, reliable. They present something trustworthy in the midst of precarious hope.[13]

The paperback cover of Berlant's *Cruel Optimism* is both striking and instructive. It is a copy of a painting by Riva Lehrer, entitled *If Body: Riva and Zora in Middle Age*. In the foreground is a dog, a German Shepherd called Zora, and

---

13 When I read a version of this paper to Concord, a theological group to which I belong, my friend Dr Kim Wasey noted that one of the concerns she had about the way I present Berlant's take is that it feels rather extreme. That is, that it presents a world in which one commits to something 'grand' and one is essentially doomed to failure. She reminded me that most of us don't live grand lives with grand projects; we set modest goals and those goals can shift in and over time. I hear the force of Wasey's point. I think Berlant might counter that even our modest goals are subject to endless accommodation and adaptation, as we are bruised and traumatized by the effects of life.

behind it lies a prone Riva, wearing a red party dress and long white opera gloves. She holds her left hand over her face as she orientates towards Zora. Zora sits looking up and away from Riva, blind in her left eye and her right seemingly mesmerized by something in the distance. She is happy perhaps. Certainly, she seems contented. Around her neck is a cone, presumably to prevent the scratching of a wound, a sore, perhaps the blind eye. Her long tail rests on Riva's hips, offering a kind of intimacy and relationship, perhaps even comfort. In her own commentary on the artwork, Berlant says:

> Riva, her face half covered, is probably weeping. But Riva is not in an absolute heap, destroyed by discomposure. She is using her hand to hold her face half-together and to touch what Zora cannot also touch. At the same time, she hides what Zora cannot also hide, so that the dog has a face for two, it seems: aimed, perhaps towards the light.[14]

Berlant draws attention to the title of the piece: '*If Body*. There is no verb, no action, only a tendency that's subjunctive, propositional. There is an IF but no THEN: and so, if one follows the IF, what does one find, then?'[15] Berlant's findings are suggestive and incredibly powerful:

> If body, pain. If body, misery. If body, attrition, vulnerability, wearing out … if body, other bodies: unseen and in proximity, abstract and untouchable. If body, imitation – Riva covers her face as though she can be blind like Zora, but the difference between being and likeness is played out a hundredfold, and she is not blind, only tender, trying to stay in synch. If body, there's Riva and Zora, hanging there and hanging in there, in the middle.[16]

---

14 Berlant, *Cruel Optimism*, pp. 265–6.
15 Berlant, *Cruel Optimism*, p. 266.
16 Berlant, *Cruel Optimism*, p. 266.

They hang in the middle of precariousness. They are inhabitants of the Third City, of the Broken Middle, indicated by Gillian Rose.[17]

Riva Lehrer lives with spina bifida. As Berlant puts it, 'Riva is riven in the middle.' However, the middle to which the title refers is middle age. Riva and Zora are two vulnerable bodies, but, as Berlant suggests:

> [They] seem at peace with each other's bodily being, and seem to have given each other what they came for: companionship, reciprocity, care, protection. Bodies make each other a little more possible: but they can't do everything ... What we do have together, in the middle of this thing, is a brush with solidarity, and that's real.[18]

These two are not – in conventional terms – normal or flourishing. But they have achieved something. They are, on Berlant's

---

17 Philosopher Gillian Rose develops the concept of the Broken Middle in *The Broken Middle: Out of Our Ancient Society* (Oxford: Wiley-Blackwell, 1992). For an analysis of this concept, see Rachel Mann, 'Presiding from the Broken Middle', in *Presiding Like a Woman: Feminist Gesture for Christians*. The Broken Middle represents the complex, lived ground or space between binaried philosophical or judicial or theoretical concepts. Rose posits it as a third term between, for example, the universal and the particular, the law and ethics, and actuality and potentiality. In Kate Schick's summary, the Broken Middle is a critique of 'the old, for its prescription and progressivism, and the new, for its rejection of the struggle to know and to judge'. See Kate Schick, *Gillian Rose: A Good Enough Justice* (Edinburgh: Edinburgh University Press, 2012), pp. 36–7, as well as Section 1, Part 2. In *Mourning Becomes the Law: Philosophy and Representation* (Cambridge: Cambridge University Press, 1996), Rose attempts to revisit the concept of the Broken Middle through the political metaphor of the City. In our European discourse, the politics of reason ('Athens') vies in tension with the politics of the idealized ethic ('New Jerusalem'); behind and between them lies the Third City, the politics through which we live. See, especially, Rose, *Mourning*, pp. 20–35. She adds, 'the difficult [...] work of the middle [...] sits between tragedy and utopia: acknowledging the profound brokenness of actuality, whilst refusing to be paralysed by this brokenness'. Schick, *Gillian Rose*, p. 37.

18 Berlant, *Cruel Optimism*, p. 266.

terms, a team and, in the midst of life's provisional, precarious terms, that's something. It has promise. If there is no real stability in life then this achievement of solidarity holds the promise of 'having adventures and being in the impasse together, waiting for the other shoe to drop, and also, allowing for some healing and resting, waiting for it not to drop'. If body, then everything can follow.

Berlant notes that this might mean that these two operate outside the limits of cruel optimism. They reciprocate and are simply present and being themselves without projection or misrecognition. They are not fantasists. Nonetheless, Berlant insists:

> even in those circumstances mortality and vulnerability hover as the velvet uncanny of the situation. Even when you get what you want, you can't have what you want. Even the best relation, the one that deserves the optimism you attach to it, can turn out cruelly when conditions beyond you or any dog's control suddenly cleave your confidence.[19]

Any of us – of faith and none – who have lived long enough will have encountered this economy at the heart of our commitments, our loves, our optimisms and our hopes. It breaks us and traumatizes our bodies and our relationships. We are exposed. Even solidarity or honest reciprocity can fail us. Still I want to say, 'Christ yesterday, Christ today, Christ for all time'. Not merely as a mantra or as a desperate gesture into the indifference or the cruelty of the universe or the precariousness of bodies in a precarious world. No. I want to do so because it captures hope rather than optimism; the hope that scopes mortality and vulnerability and holds them in the Body of Christ.

There is a moving 'adjacency' about Riva and Zora; their adjacent precariousness engenders a solidarity. They barely touch, but they touch. But God invites us into more than adjacent bodies; we are invited to be indwelling bodies ... this is

---

19 Berlant, *Cruel Optimism*, pp. 266–7.

not the temporary indwelling of sexual intimacy, ever riven with the threat and possibility of exploitation and violence. This is the God placed in our hands in bread and wine, flesh and blood, on whom we feast.

In short, all our optimisms break in the face of death and violence and vulnerability. We cannot make ourselves safe. We cannot close the story happily. But that's not the Christian hope. The Christian hope requires not only the embrace of our structural precarities, but finds them necessary for life. Only through death – the small deaths and the great death – can we find our way to life. This is not a fetishization of death and fragility and precariousness. It is full recognition, but it is also an embrace of God's way shown through Christ. Not cheap victory, but a victory in the midst of trauma and wound.

In *Wartime*, Fussell quotes this line written by the poet Stephen Spender in September 1939: 'What are we fighting for? Personally, I think we ought to be fighting a kind of defensive rearguard action against the development of absolutely chaotic and brutal conditions.'[20] Perhaps – in a world of cruelty, where our stratagems of improvement and goodness so often seem to come to naught – that is the best we can offer. Perhaps we should seek after the moving adjacency of Riva and Zora. Or, perhaps, in the riches of the Christian vision we behold something else and more: in the midst of the threat of absolutely chaotic and brutal conditions one continues to model grace and fearless friendship and a willingness to conform one's own life to Christ's abiding sacrifice for all.

---

20 Fussell, *Wartime*, p. 134.

8

The Precarious Word

George Herbert begins his poem 'The Windows' with a decep-
tively simple question: 'Lord, how can man preach thy eternall
word?' It is a question that should bring up short all those
called to preach. For, as this book has sought to explore, there
is a beautiful, pathetic and sometimes tragic precariousness
in human being. How might this frail human frame speak,
preach and model God's eternal love? As Herbert himself puts
it, humanity is 'a brittle crazie glass'. It may seem constitutionally beyond us to speak the story of God which God seeks to
'anneal in glass', in trust and hope that 'light and glorie/ More
rev'rend grows'. God is no brittle glass. He is the unmediated
light of the universe, too bright for us.

In the midst of our brittleness, it is not unreasonable that
the notion of God's eternal word might bring great comfort to
many Christians, especially in troublous and precarious times.
Indeed, has it not been the case that in the midst of the changing scenes of life, Scripture – as the word of God – has been the
rock? It is earth so refined and fired that it has become rock.
Isn't that one of the gifts of the Psalms, say? They direct us to
God, but also sing God, the Living Word:

> The Lord *is* my rock, and my fortress, and my deliverer;
> my God, my strength, in whom I will trust.[1]

We – as earth creatures, as dust made life – long for the deeper
earth of God:

---

1 Psalm 18.2a.

My soul cleaveth unto the dust:
quicken thou me according to thy word ...[2]

We are, at best, badly refracting glass and dim mirrors, but the word of God represents the unshakeable basis of a faith that proclaims Christ yesterday, today and tomorrow. It contains, as the Church of England's Ordinal has it, all that is necessary for salvation. We may be flesh, but Scripture is solid ground. It sets – for many Protestants at least – the bounds for what it is possible for Christians to believe. The word – the Bible – always gestures towards *the* Word: Christ. As dust creatures we are directed always to the rock who is God; as creatures of glass – of worn sand – we are sent back to the rock from which our eroded and transformed bodies emerge.

The longing for solidity – for solid ground – is surely as old as human culture. The philosopher Luce Irigaray reminds us that 'metaphysics always supposes, in some manner, a solid crust from which to raise a construction'.[3] Her discussion of this claim, centred on Martin Heidegger's analysis of Being and Clearing, as well as ancient Greek ideas about the four elements, is challenging and technical. This is not the place to get choked up with a heavy technical analysis of Heidegger, who is impenetrable at the best of times. Rather, what's fascinating is how accurately Irigaray diagnoses the longing in metaphysics, in religion and in life more broadly understood for something solid on which to raise something: 'God is my Rock', 'The World is all that is the case ...', 'In the beginning was the Word ...' 'Here I stand, I can do no other...'

Irigaray is interesting because she invites her reader to consider whether the 'solid', the 'ground' or 'matter' is ever sufficient in itself for our constructions: our desire for an intellectual, metaphysical and theological architecture. As with so many Continental philosophers, she wants to draw attention to what is concealed or ignored when we fixate on one aspect. She invites

---

2 Psalm 119.25.
3 Luce Irigaray, *The Forgetting of Air in Martin Heidegger*, trans. Mary Beth Mader (London: The Athlone Press, 1999 (1983)), p. 2.

us to consider 'air' as a necessary and ignored counterpoint to
the human philosophical and intellectual tendency to focus on
'the material', on 'solidity' and 'matter'. Air represents – for
Irigaray – 'appearance, expression, mime, to appear, to seem,
to resemble ... And even: a piece of music written for solo voice,
accompanying lyrics; a tune.'[4] Air can seem ephemeral, passing, unseen; forgettable and impermanent. Readily dismissed
as temporary. Unstable. Precarious – and therefore unworthy
of close attention.

Perhaps it would be helpful if, for non-philosophical readers,
I put the above in slightly different, theological terms. One
place to consider – as I have repeatedly in this book – is the
myth of Adam and Eve. In the second creation story, *Ha'adam*
is formed from the earth. From the dust. From the obviously
'this-worldly', the material. However, to become fully alive the
earth creature must receive the breath of God. The obviously
material – earth, matter, solidity – is insufficient in itself; the
breath of God – mystery, a song, unseen, still real and strangely
material – supplies the sufficiency in relationship with the
obviously material.

I suppose I want, then, to draw attention to how our metaphors and stories open up and close down our ways of reading
a changing, precarious world. When one talks of God 'our
Rock' or the 'Eternal Word' one can feel that one is offering a
bulwark against a precarious world, based in a kind of unques-
tionable and unbreakable metaphysics. In this metaphysical
picture, the 'word of God' offers a 'sure foundation' against
the 'Spirit of the Age, which is like the wind'. Here is the solid
ground of our being beyond the vicissitudes of time and space.
Herein shall air – in Irigaray's terms – not touch.

The concept and metaphor of air is not alien to the Christian
faith, of course, though it may trouble us. When a thinker
like Irigaray invites her readers to consider the 'metaphysics'
of air and its meanings, it may strike Christians as just one
more postmodern and post-structural attempt to 'historicize'
everything. For, by drawing attention to the significations of

---

4 Irigaray, *The Forgetting*, p. 5.

air – its instability, its seeming invisibility, its precariousness – some Christians may worry that the likes of Irigaray just want to be destructive. Where Christians may wish to talk of God or Scripture or the Word as metaphysically sure – 'solid', 'rock-like', 'eternal' – the likes of Irigaray want to expose such terms as necessarily contingent.[5]

Perhaps where Christian tradition is most at ease with the possible meanings – metaphorical and otherwise – of air is in representations of the Holy Spirit. The Spirit presents, in one sense, the most elusive person of the Godhead. For the Father and the Son rely in part, for their power, on human analogues. Not so the Spirit. In the Tanakh, God's Spirit is represented as *ruah* or *ruach*, the breath of God. In Genesis 1.2, the Spirit moves over the face of the waters; in Genesis 2.7, God breathes life into the dust of the earth creature, bringing life. In the New Testament, arguably the defining 'air'-based image is found in Acts 2, the account of the apostles being filled with the Spirit on the day of Pentecost. Here the Spirit – *pneuma* – is characterized as a rushing wind and like a fire. In John's Gospel, the Spirit is described as like a wind blowing where it will: 'thou hearest the sound thereof, but canst not tell whence it cometh, and whither it goeth'.[6] In other places, one finds representations of the Spirit as like water, dove and fire.

The Spirit is not reducible to any or all of these things; the Spirit always leads people into metaphor and, therefore, into play (including the play of signs). While I would not want to deny the materiality of the biblical representations of the Spirit (wind, water, fire etc. are physical phenomena), what is exciting is how they play with the ephemeral and precarious; as with the dove itself, there is a sense in which each is a creature of air.

---

5 In her analysis of Heidegger's account of Being, Irigaray draws attention to his use of the concept of the Clearing. In essence, she notes how even for someone like Heidegger with such a profound and detailed account of the foundational riches and solidities of Being needs to make space for Space and Openness, for *Lichtung*/Lighting – for the Clearing in which *da-sein*, 'Being-as', or human being, is actually possible.

6 John 3.8.

It is tempting to offer an instrumental account of the Spirit. This is a picture of her work in which she simply directs us towards the solid foundation: towards Christ and through Christ to the Father. This would be a picture of the Spirit as a kind of auxiliary Person of the Godhead. She is, of course, so much more. In the Nicene Creed, the Spirit is called 'the Lord, the Giver of Life', and it is clear in New Testament discourse that she is, by turns, Comforter, Conceiver and Caller into Life. She has been, in some Protestant theologies, the Person of the Godhead with the interpretative authority to interpret Scripture in truth. As the dove that hovers, she proclaims, signals, declares and directs. As fire, she sets the faithful alive with God. She calls the oppressed into liberation and she exposes and connects God's people to the power at the heart of the universe.

In John 3, Jesus says to the old man and leader, Nicodemus:

Verily, verily, I say unto thee, Except a man be born of water and *of* the Spirit, he cannot enter into the kingdom of God ... The wind bloweth where it listeth, and thou hearest the sound thereof, but canst not tell whence it cometh, and whither it goeth: so is every one that is born of the Spirit.[7]

Here Jesus is addressing Nicodemus' reasonable concerns about who Jesus might be and what participating in the kingdom might look like. Jesus famously says that to enter the kingdom of God a person must be 'born again' or 'born from above' – in short, born of the Spirit. One of the exciting dimensions of this passage is how the Spirit – as air and wind – dislodges the fixity of our fleshly births. We cannot, in the kingdom of God, rely on what we imagine has already been achieved – via our birth, our status, our seemingly already rehearsed and self-evident identities. The Spirit is disruptive. She breaks through and breaks up our reliance on one kind of solidity: 'flesh'. If, in theological terms and Christian tradition, 'flesh' should not simply be treated as equivalent to 'body', here is a

---

7 John 3.5–8.

striking moment of disruption in the human tendency to want solid ground. In Nicodemus' case it is the solid ground of lived, common sense: he makes an indisputable claim – no one can re-enter the womb. Jesus' reminder of the nature of the Spirit is a challenge to anyone, including me, who might be tempted to fetishize what is obvious and sure in our material culture. It is as true today as in Jesus' time that no one can re-enter the womb or – to push the point – be raised from the dead. That's not how flesh and body works. Except in the economy of God. The Holy Spirit lives to shock.

More than that, Christ indicates that at God's profoundest reality – the Godhead – there is this utterly disruptive lack of solidity. At the point of metaphysical solidity there is air. There is movement and perichoresis. God the Father and God the Son are not afraid of this. Nor should we be. We should not be afraid of the play and possibility and the mystery. The Spirit makes things happen. Indeed, this play has implications for how we treat with both the living Word of God, Christ, and the scriptural word of God. Consider the mystery of Christ's conception. When Gabriel visits Mary in the Annunciation, and tells her she will conceive God's Son:

> Then said Mary unto the angel, How shall this be, seeing I know not a man? And the angel answered and said unto her, The Holy Ghost shall come upon thee, and the power of the Highest shall overshadow thee: therefore also that holy thing which shall be born of thee shall be called the Son of God.[8]

Many, including me, have explored in other contexts the extent to which this might be a scene of rape.[9] Here I want to examine this as a scene of consensual disruption of the world's economy: as a meeting point of 'air' and 'flesh'; of 'spirit' and 'dust'. The 'holy thing' born of Mary is precisely the meeting point of dust and air, met in the site of 'compassion', the womb. Holy has implications of intactness and wholeness and

---

8 Luke 1.34–35.
9 See, for example, Rachel Mann, *Dazzling Darkness* (Glasgow: Wild Goose, 2012), chapter 8.

inviolability.[10] Thingness has implications of 'assemblage' (of persons), the pitiable and the material. In God's economy, the conception of Christ brings together the inviolably 'pure' and whole – the completeness and oneness of God – with that which is pitched into the world as an assemblage of parts, of cells and limbs and organs. The Holy Thing which is Christ is both made and for all time; is matter and air.

On this picture I've sketched, it is air that is more substantial and whole than the stuff of dust and matter. It is a subversion of traditional metaphysics and it is, as such, rather marvellous. Air, spirit, fire is not to be readily controlled and can seem precarious and unstable. Yet it is the wholeness at the heart of the world, which dares to be pitched – in thingness, in body, in flesh – into the precarity we live and know. It is the inviolate God who is prepared to be violated by our violence. It is the self-offering Love in all things which seems barely there – spotted in a first-century Jewish peasant, and found in communities of solidarity and trust, made available in bread and wine – and is more solid than all the things of this world in which one is inclined to place one's trust.

There is a beauty and a potential tragedy in this risky openness found in the Living God. The beauty lies in the way that openness creates space for the whole of humanity to find their lives, loves and promise within the Godhead. The beauty is found in the openness. The tragedy, however, emerges out of our unwillingness to accept and rejoice in the Word's open texture. So often we want of the Word – of Christ, of Scripture – a level of fixity that does a disservice to the Word's living reality. Whether it be the Church, or its denominations or a tradition, there can be this urge or compulsion to say, 'This! This is what this passage definitively means', or a hunger to nail Christ to a doctrinal position from which he can never escape. And then the Word – the words of Scripture, the body of Christ – comes alive, and slips away into unexpected meanings and significations. The body that we have nailed to

---

10 I suspect it is partly through this (potentially creepy) lineage that Mary's status as *Parthenos* – a girl – has been transmuted to holy virgin.

doctrine dies and, to our alarm, rises again. And we have to fight our urge to force the body back on its cross or the word into its pre-prepared meaning.

The living Word is always animated by the Spirit. Air and flame flow and flare, and sometimes we catch a glimpse of her on our breath, as if she is most known to us when we go out for a walk on a frosty morning. Then we grasp it: God is no idol, fixed by us for our purposes. She exceeds and disturbs and distresses us. If she does not, how else could she be the hope for the world? How else could she be adequate to a world that is necessarily and sacredly precarious? How else could she meet our urge to reduce this open-textured, hallowed world to the banal, the regular, the predictable? The already achieved and rehearsed? As I shall explore in the next chapter, we can fear the unseen and the unpredictable. The uncanny and odd. Like a virus passed around unknowingly, the Spirit can cause alarm. In one sense, she should. She should because she is more faithful and kind and compassionate and generous than we dare believe. She will not kill us, though things within us may yet die.

In my recent poem sequence, *A Kingdom of Love*, which meditates on the work of a priest, I include a poem, 'The Book of Genesis':

> Before holy or righteous, before the Law,
> Before sound was distilled (so many crossings-out)
> Into *bet, aleph, niqqud*, before all that: Song.
>
> Oh, to taste fricatives – damp from lip and palate –
> Dental trills, the Spirit chewed by teeth,
> Ejected from lungs, an offering.
>
> Oh, to know before, before, before the Book: Decision.
> Should the Fruit be plucked or crushed?
> And, love, what place love?[11]

This poem imagines a time before the Law, before word was written, before the mystery of Scripture was laid down; it

11 Rachel Mann, *A Kingdom of Love* (Manchester: Carcanet Press, 2019), p. 8.

imagines time before time; it offers the Spirit up to the primal moment. It dares to imagine a picture of Spirit – of air and breath – so fundamental to body that it can be chewed by teeth, ejected from lungs, an offering. This is the wild Spirit participating in time and space, caught up in the love of the universe which calls life from Life. This is the Spirit that remains available to us; not as the one who trumps the Law or overmasters Scripture, but who invites us into the deeper life of the Body of Christ flowing through the Law and Scripture and completing them.

To participate in the Body of Christ is to participate in the life of the Spirit. As the Body breathes in and out, it breathes the wild air of God, the Spirit of life. Indeed, I think at a profound level, the Eucharist is the lungs of the Church, breathing in and out the love of God and remaking the world. In calling us to Eucharist, the priest invites us to feast on Christ in spirit and truth; in physical form, as bread and wine. We are, as the Body, then sent out into the world for the world to feast on us through our service and love. When we break bread and share wine outpoured, the Spirit breathes new life through and in the community of God. The breaking of the bread, the piercing of Christ's body, is paradoxically a moment of breath. The lungs of Jesus' body are clogged with water and blood and the soldier pierces them. We thrust our weapons in. Blood and water pour out, and God breathes anew. When we feast on the body and blood of Christ, we feast on a pierced body that releases its final breath, the last drop of oxygen from a destroyed body into the world, for the sake of the world. We feast on flesh, and mess, and blood; we receive air. We are oxygenated by God. We take his breath out into the world. And the world breathes. And in the dark, God waits to be raised to new life.

9

How the Grotesque Speaks
to the Precarious Body

In this penultimate chapter I want to give some thought to the
idea of the 'grotesque' and what it might mean if to be human
entails, in a certain sense, being grotesque; I want to examine how the grotesque might relate to precarious bodies, both
God's and ours, and, crucially, how the grotesque – ironically
– might be a site of hope and joy in this precarious world.

I suspect that were one to be called 'grotesque' by another
or labelled as such by a community or by society, one might
be horrified. It is not a word that typically has terribly positive
associations. The word or concept has associations of ugliness
and something of the ridiculous. The kind of situation one
might consider 'grotesque' is – to use modern vernacular
– likely to be a situation that 'grosses people out'. It will be
repellent and offensive. If one were confronted with a decaying dead body or the chewed-up remains of a pet crushed
by a motor car, one might reasonably describe the vision as
'grotesque'. Perhaps if one thought about the sheer profligacy
with which some people spend money one might describe such
conspicuous consumption as 'grotesque'.

There is a sense in which the grotesque goes beyond lines of
decency. And because of that there is – properly read – a kind
of ridiculousness that can generate giddiness and laughter and
mockery. This effect may not strike us as especially 'tasteful' –
indeed, it is not – but it remains a common reaction to much
that is grotesque. The human or the situation or object that is
designated as grotesque can produce a dark line of humour.
Why? Because, from the point of view of the 'normal', the

grotesque's transgression simply looks 'odd', 'incongruous' or bizarre. The grotesque's excess is the excess demonstrated in the realm of the freak show and the burlesque and the monstrous inhuman. It is not beautiful or pleasing. It can be distressing and vile. It can be exploitative. It can be as horrible and compelling as a public execution.

Patrick Parrinder, in his study of the work of James Joyce, reminds us that the word *grotesque* 'derives from a type of Roman ornamental design first discovered in the fifteenth century, during the excavation of Titus's baths'.[1] Named after the 'grottos' in which they were found, the forms found mixed human and animal designs, blended with fruit and foliage in such ways that classical art ideas were subverted. Parrinder quotes Vitruvius' contemporary 'take-down' of this 'style' of art, in his *On Architecture*:

> Such things neither are, nor can be, nor have been ... For how can a reed actually sustain a roof, or a candelabrum the ornament of a gable? Or a soft and slender stalk a seated statue? Or how can flowers and half-statues rise alternately from roots and stalks? Yet when people view these false-hoods, they approve rather than condemn, failing to consider whether any of them can really occur or not.

If we might find Vitruvius' analysis of the grotesque rather too hidebound, too 'realist' and tied to almost totalitarian conceptions of the visual, he notes how – even in classical contexts – there is something appealing about grotesque things. They draw us as they repel. Very often the way they draw us is via laughter. They might be read as 'witty' and 'amusing'.

The cultural critic Mark Fisher explores this simultaneous repel–attract/horror–laughter horizon of the grotesque in his analysis of the Manchester rock band The Fall, notably their 1980 album *Grotesque (After the Gramme)*. This is an album characterized by incongruous musical styles – punk, New

---

1 Patrick Parrinder, *James Joyce* (Cambridge: Cambridge University Press, 1984), p. 8.

Wave, *krautrock*, modernism, rockabilly – coming together and falling apart. The lyrics too ('huckleberry masks', 'light-blue plant heads') are surreal and only begin to make sense when read through the grotesque juxtapositions outlined in Parrinder's notes on Vitruvius. The tracks themselves are deliberately badly recorded, drawing attention to the making of the record or, as Fisher puts it, 'brandished like improvised stitching on some Hammer Frankenstein monster'.[2] On the track 'Impression of J Temperance', a dog breeder's purple-eyed 'hideous replica' stalks Manchester in music that is so silted up it might have been dredged up from the Ship Canal.

Fisher notes that this grotesque music generates laughter: it is 'a renegade form of parody and mockery that one hesitates to call satire'.[3] However, he suggests:

With The Fall ... it is as if satire is returned to its origins in the grotesque. The Fall's laughter does not issue from the commonsensical mainstream but from a psychotic outside ... a [psycho]tropological spewing of associations and animosities, the true object of which is not any failing of probity but the delusion that human dignity is possible.[4]

Indeed, Fisher makes the startling claim that in the wild, irruptive picture of the world found in the grotesque – gestured towards by the strange juxtapositions of The Fall's 'art' and the alien combinations that resist classical ideas of form – one discovers:

It is the human condition to be grotesque, since the human animal is the one that does not fit in, the freak of nature who has no place in the natural order and is capable of re-combining nature's products into hideous new forms.[5]

---

2 Mark Fisher, *The Weird and the Eerie* (London: Repeater Books, 2016), p. 34.
3 Fisher, *The Weird*, p. 34.
4 Fisher, *The Weird*, p. 35.
5 Fisher, *The Weird*, p. 34.

How is Christianity to engage with the grotesque? I think this matters not least because the grotesque seems so readily available in human culture, and story. The grotesque is a feature of our bodies. I know it is tempting to treat the grotesque as an aberration or a mistake; it is tempting to act as if it is something that is avoidable or readily corrected. However, if Fisher is correct, to be grotesque is to be human; we are a kind of living, flesh anomaly with a genius to combine nature's productions into hideous new forms. In one sense, that toying with, celebration of, and transgression of 'limit' represents a line through which art and culture itself is produced. Indeed, part of what makes Fisher's analysis of The Fall so intriguing – from a Christian point of view – is the band's very name. There is a sense in which even at the level of name, Mark E. Smith's outfit – intentionally or subconsciously – embodies the cosmic demarcation that Christianity both posits and addresses: the Fall.

Perhaps the grotesque matters because it speaks into the precariousness of our bodies and lived realities. When we are 'grossed-out' by the grotesque or we feel we can do nothing but laugh in the face of it, we acknowledge the strange and radical wildness in the midst of and beyond the ways we live. Certainly, those reactions indicate a desire to distance oneself from grotesquery. However, the desire to generate distance is a reaffirmation of the grotesque's proximity. The grotesque reminds us that we cannot simply make things neat and judicious and safe, or keep the wild frontiers of 'unsanity' and transgression bounded. This is, in no way, a justification of mockery or an apologia for the freak show in which people point or laugh at those marked down as 'other' or 'different'. Rather, it is as if the more one desires to demonstrate one's probity, one's sense and normality, the more the human gift for 'unsense', nonsense and transgression is delineated. This transgression might, by turns, be coded as wickedness or brilliance, criminality or art; it might be coded as grotesquery or offence.

In one sense, Christianity holds the grotesque within its foundational being; it is a ground of what gives the faith life and energy and shape. The grotesque is a horizon of Christianity's transformation of the site of a murder into the very Tree of Life.[6] Killing God using an instrument of torture reserved for a criminal is arguably an icon of grotesquery. Christian sublimations of the act of killing a man – Jesus – into the killing of God produce the extraordinary representation of the World Tree growing up-through human flesh, just as (representative) human flesh is turned into the World Tree. It is paradoxical and mysterious and offensive. It is impossible, yet possible. Indeed, there is a sense in which it defies 'representation' at all. The cross is absence and the nihil. It is God – emptied into human flesh – murdered. Yet it is represented as life: the Tree of Life at the heart of Eden is cast on a rubbish dump – on Calvary – and it descends to Gehenna and grows again, for it is the true Tree.

I have never quite recovered from my face-to-face encounter with various states of the 'print in etching' by Rembrandt known variously as *The Three Crosses* or *Christ Between Two Thieves*. In it we witness not only Christ and the criminals he is crucified alongside, but the Blessed Virgin, St John, Roman soldiers and a crowd of witnesses. Christ is at the centre and, in the earliest versions of the print, Christ is suffused with light. What is extraordinary is how the various stages of printing, over a period of ten or so years, generate progressively more disturbing, chaotic and shadowed effects. As Rembrandt aged and delved into the moment of Christ's death, he seemed to expose the viewer ever more to the grotesquery that lurks at the heart of our salvation.

In *The Three Crosses*, it is as if the darkness gestures towards the 'unrepresentability' of the cross and, by implication, of Christ's work of salvation. In the final state, the Blessed Virgin seems to be almost a disembodied head surrounded by darkness. In each state of the print, Christ is always at the centre. In the early versions his centrality is utterly suffused by light.

---

6 For a fascinating spiritual study of the cross as Tree of Life, see Gonville Ffrench-Beytagh, *Tree of Glory* (London: Darton, Longman and Todd, 1988).

However, by the final phase of the etching such light as there is, is a kind of dazzling darkness that illumines the mystery of God's love. In the shadows, God is at work. Indeed, in this precarious world, perhaps that's the only place from which salvation can come. It is mystery, it is practically unrepresentable. Perhaps one might even push this further and claim that there is deeper, theological fact which prevents this representation: the very notion of the hypostatic union of divine and human nature, modelled in *The Three Crosses*, is a work of the grotesque; it is a work of offence and transgression.

I suspect Christian treatments of the grotesque are likely to be offensive to contemporary, post-Christian critical tastes not least because those treatments typically mythologize it. Indeed, there are many within Christianity itself who find the mythologized aesthetics of the cross too much like glorification. The cross is hideous – a work of human manufacture that transmutes nature into something with one vile end: a tortured death. It is a gross and obscene mode of murder that deprives its victims of any dignity and is designed to humiliate and punish. There are those who have sought – especially from liberationist and feminist perspectives – to emphasize the cross as representing less of a divine means of reconciliation between God and humanity and more of an exposure of the worst of human abusiveness and violence.[7] On these accounts, if the cross's value lies in anything it is in its invitation to live differently. To mythologize the cross as having cosmic significance, according to these theologies, is to betray what Christ is inviting us towards.[8]

Nonetheless, the mythological and the grotesque meet in Christianity. It is fascinating, for example, to consider the very notion of growing into the likeness of Christ as a moment in the grotesque. In its common use, the idea of a person 'growing

---

7 See, for example, the recent popular article by Professors Katie Edwards and David Tombs on Christ as a victim of sexual abuse: https://shiloh-project.group.shef.ac.uk/himtoo-why-jesus-should-be-recognised-as-a-victim-of-sexual-violence/ (accessed: 24.03.2020).

8 Consider, for example, positions developed by Kosuke Koyama, René Girard and James Allison, among others.

into the likeness of Christ' may come across as a highly refined, sophisticated theological claim, a development of centuries of exhortations and invitations by the Church to 'put on the Lord Jesus Christ'.[9] One might read this notion as – in metaphorical terms – a kind of divine 'dressing up'.[10]

However, for all the childlike innocence of the notion of 'dressing up', the idea of 'putting on the Lord Jesus Christ' also has implications of acting, performance and performativity, indeed of living or acting out an identity or a role. 'Acting' – even in the positive Aristotelian sense in which one forms virtuous habits by acting as if one has those habits – is an activity that always runs the risk of the grotesque. At the edges of its performances always lies the possibility of excessive fakery, and luridness and the parodic. It always risks the absurd mockery that some see in drag's representation of femininity. Indeed, there are modes of Christianity that have always been suspicious of theatre and acting's capacity to falsify and fake: its willingness to conceal and play through face paint, or create fake palaces made out of canvas. The actor always risks becoming grotesque by over-playing her role. There is a line of transgression in performance which scares some religious people: the move from 'who we are' to 'who we imagine ourselves to be'. It is the line that has been policed for centuries by those of faith who fear gender and sexual 'outlaws'. But, ironically, Christianity has its own 'legitimate' version of the 'transgression': to be our 'true' selves we must become more like Jesus than we are ever ourselves. We move beyond what is given to what we can be in completeness: more like the only complete human, Jesus Christ. Jesus Christ who was grotesquely violated and carries the marks of that violation into his glorious resurrection.

In his recent film set in the Great War, *1917*, Sir Sam Mendes creates a kinetic, hallucinatory and immersive examination of

---

9 Romans 13.14.

10 For a fascinating study of the significance of clothes and clothing metaphors in the Bible, see Frances Shaw, *Wearing Well: Exploring the Biblical Imagery of Clothing* (Vancouver: Regent College Publishing, 2019).

the impact of war on human relationship, bodies and flesh. In many respects it does not – as a complete piece of work – belong to the category of the grotesque. Unlike the intertwining of impossible things found in The Fall's work, Mendes brings a carefully aestheticized rendering of war. This is signalled not least by the immersive and tasteful use of Thomas Newman's music, which saturates the film. Mendes is not afraid of trauma and the irruption of violence as such. Indeed, it is absolutely front and centre in much of the film's remarkable achievement; however, because there is a sense in which 1917 belongs to the category of quest – and therefore of romance – it holds the grotesque in check.

For this is – at the most obvious level – a film that centres on a young man's quest to stop the grotesque overwhelming what remains of human order: family, duty, the regiment as an ordered body of men. A young soldier, Blake, is commissioned to head far beyond the front line in order to stop an advanced British regiment from slaughtering itself in the mistaken belief that it has 'the Hun on the run'. The driver for this young soldier – and the emotional motor for the film – is that he has a brother who is an officer in the regiment that is about to go over the top. Ultimately, though there is trauma and horror along the way, and it is not completed without intense personal cost and violence, the mission is accomplished. In that respect, the grotesque represented by war is seen off. It is (that most non-grotesque category) 'managed'. In short, the story arc offers a conservative response to the catastrophe of war, at least, within the frame of the film.

However, I'm not sure it's quite that simple. Though human dignity and conservative family relationships are broadly restated at the end of the film, Mendes does not entirely side-step the suggestion made by Mark Fisher that the human condition is grotesque, 'since the human animal is the one that does not fit in, the freak of nature who has no place in the natural order and is capable of re-combining nature's products into hideous new forms'.[11] Mendes's picture of war rehearses

---

11 Fisher, The Weird, p. 35.

the strange juxtapositions of the grotesque at various points. Here is a world in which earth and root grow through human flesh, and human bodies become 'navigation tools' through a land where the flowers are barbed wire. Corpses have melted into earth and bones are as commonplace as seeds.

This is a world where humans destroy their own habitat – burning down churches and houses – and are forced to live in mud pits for safety. It is a world represented so potently in those works of Otto Dix, where men are reduced to monsters in masks or mere purpling meat. Crucially, this state of war, represented in *1917* and so many cultural representations of the Great War, is grotesque because it reveals precisely how much the human animal does not fit. The human animal takes 'nature' – its material facts, and products – and recombines them into the hideous; this creature is so obscene that it uses nature's products and materials to destroy itself. Of course, this is not merely what humans are, but in light of our genius for exploiting and destroying our environment and damaging the planet, it is difficult to resist the conclusion that war simply represents us in particular, uncontrolled circumstances.

The film *1917* – for all its flaws – arguably presents a Christian response to the grotesquery at the centre of our being. It presents an account of the sacralization or mythologization of the grotesque that is analogous to the mythos of the cross. The grotesquery of the trenches might appear to be mere background for a quest, a kind of prop that functions to foreground the power of a quest to save thousands of lives and, for Blake, to save his brother among them. However, the film's romance and quest elements never overwhelm the grotesque; the grotesque remains part of the quest, at best held back for another day. This is demonstrated not only in the fate of Blake himself, but of his pal Schofield.

Blake is set up as the hero of the film. He is asked to go out beyond – not simply into – no man's land in order to save his brother; armed only with his gift for memorizing maps and immense courage, he heads out on this mission which will ultimately save thousands of others from death in a doomed attack on new German lines. He chooses his friend Schofield, a veteran of the Somme and decorated hero, as his pal on his quest. Early in their journey, Blake saves Schofield from death, and guides him half-blind from the site of danger. Through that action alone, Blake has demonstrated he is a hero.

It is at this point that *1917* subverts the viewer's expectations and refuses to hold back the grotesque any longer. While taking respite in an abandoned farm, Schofield finds a single signal of human civilization: a pail of fresh milk, taken from the only remaining cow (dozens of others have been slaughtered to prevent the allies from using them to live off). He tastes it and it is good, and he fills his water bottle with it. It is a moment of sweetness. Almost immediately, a dogfight breaks out above Blake and Schofield, and the German plane is shot down. It crashes into the outhouse Schofield had been standing in moments before and bursts into flames. The pilot is still alive and begins to burn to death. Once again, Blake steps forward and with Schofield saves the poor pilot. While Blake looks after the pilot on the ground, Schofield goes to find some water. At this moment, everything changes: the pilot stabs Blake, the man who saved him, in the stomach, Schofield shoots the pilot and – in a sequence of simultaneous deep distress and strange tenderness – Blake bleeds to death.

The first time I saw *1917*, I found myself sobbing uncontrollably as Blake died. As a viewer one is moved, in the space of a few seconds, from thinking, 'Oh, this will be fine, Schofield will save him, it will be a flesh wound,' to recognizing that Blake is bleeding out. His skin tone moves from ruddy to blue. He asks Schofield to write to his mother. He hallucinates that the sparks from the plane's fire is snow. It is a study in precariousness and the ugly. It is shattering. It makes the viewer recognize how quickly flesh is made into meat and how readily the hero – in conditions of the grotesque – is turned into an abandoned body. Schofield takes one set of Blake's dog tags and leaves his body among the anonymous dead, just one more body. The German pilot, who only moments before had also been a man with a story and a life, perhaps a sweetheart, is also abandoned on the ground with no more dignity than the cattle his colleagues shot hours before.

Out of this grotesque precarity, Schofield – who has disavowed heroism as a result of what he saw on the Somme – is forced to step forward and become the hero of the quest. On his way to find Blake's brother and the lost battalions, he saves a baby with the milk he found, and – in a genuinely striking and hallucinatory sequence – he ends up escaping a burning town that is a vision of the *Inferno*. As he runs from German soldiers, he launches himself into a river and, as he flows on his back downriver, blossom falls on him, an echo of the sparks that fell on Blake like snow. It is a moment where beauty is seemingly restored. It is a moment of pastoral – a reminder that behind the sites of war, nature waits – which has echoes of the aesthetics of Rivendell in *Lord of the Rings*. This is a world of magic and fantasy. Perhaps everything is going to be all right. Then, Schofield floats into a dam. It is made of bloated human bodies.

Still there is time for Schofield to save everyone. He climbs out of the river and finds the soldiers who are about to go over the top. One sings a plaintive version of the old folk song, 'Wayfaring Stranger'. It is a moment where holy longing breaks into the action. These are soldiers who are resigned to duty and death. They have embraced the grotesque as necessary. They sense that the only home left to them now lies over Jordan, in heaven. However, through a work of outrageous heroism/ desperation, Schofield runs into no man's land again, weaving in and out of the advancing soldiers. Eventually he finds the senior commander and manages to stop the attack after the first wave. Nonetheless, dozens are killed for nothing and hundreds more injured and maimed. In the midst of the tragedy, however, Blake's brother – a lieutenant who'd been in the first wave – is found. He is alive, tending to his troops. Schofield – who by this time is more scarecrow than man, more corpse than soldier, who is a walking trauma – delivers the news of his pal Blake's death and obtains permission from Blake's brother to write to the family. Schofield walks off, finds a tree under which to sit, and takes out a photo. It is of his family. He has kept it hidden throughout the film.

Arguably, this is a conservative ending which suggests that

order and good form has been re-established in the midst of the grotesque. Schofield sits beneath a tree and takes out his reminder of a world without the grotesque: his photo of his wife and daughters. The place where he finds to sit is unsullied. On the evidence of this little touch of unsullied earth, the promise of a return to the natural order remains possible, perhaps even assured. The tree is strong and grants Schofield, the raggedy man, strength and support.

However, it is not that simple. I cannot believe that the tree is incidental. Rather, it is profoundly symbolic. The tree might be Yggdrasil the World Tree, or the Tree of Life, the Tree of Christ. While Schofield finds a moment of respite, the war is not over. His achievement is provisional, and there remains nearly two years of war before any kind of 'normality' returns. Schofield is, arguably, a Christ figure who has taken the grotesque into himself – who has travelled down into the land of the dead – and who grows back up through the tree. He sees the promise of resurrection in his family. But can he ever be the same?

More to the point, he has been so traumatized and so exposed to the grotesque within that he is left wondering if he were ever that person in the photograph. He is caught between. He is a soldier and he is no longer one. He certainly doesn't look like one any more. He is rags. He has lost his belt, as if he has been placed under court martial. He looks, then, like he is under judgement. He has become a human no man's land: he has done good, but he has been obscene. This is the saviour figure found in *1917*. He has faced precariousness and knows its shape and character. He has embraced it and still glimpses the possibility of a better life. However, as he travels on – after the quest, as it were – there is a woundedness that seemingly will never heal. The grotesque will never depart. Indeed, to return to the idea of 'putting on Christ', if Schofield – in saving others – has done so, he has been exposed to wounds and brutality that have transformed him. He holds up the 'image' of himself, his wife and kids and does not know if what he sees in the picture is himself. Has he become more himself in participating in trauma and violence, or less? Certainly, he has saved others, but has he effectively destroyed himself in doing so? In the film, we do not get to find out what his resurrection, if he has one, might look like. If the photo he holds up were a mirror, it only shows himself very dimly. In becoming more Christlike, the grotesque has leeched deep into his bones.

The representation of the grotesque in *1917* is, in many ways, hardly original. It draws on tropes found in Great War writings and in 'war art' more broadly understood. From Edmund Blunden through to David Jones, there is a kind of lived hauntology in which the grotesqueness of violence and the unnatural suffuses many of their works. In Blunden's case, as Robyn Marsack notes, his very last poem was made in response to revisiting the old battlefields of the Western Front.[12] Jones, on the other hand, brings together the mythic, the holy and the grotesque in both his major works, *In Parenthesis* and *The Anathemata*. What *1917* offers, in a fresh way, is a visual representation of how these dynamics of the mythic, holy and grotesque weave in and out of human precariousness. It is – as I've sought to show, again and again – only through the body that the promise of God is ultimately found, and it is through the body that the mythic, holy and grotesque is negotiated. This is the place Christ knows and transforms.

Before the final battle in *1917*, a single soldier sings the song 'Wayfaring Stranger' while his company listens.[13] 'Wayfaring Stranger' is, in essence, a gospel song framed by a vision of travelling home to God. The soldier sings plaintively and acapella. He sings solo, but his song is every soldier's song. He is 'a poor wayfaring stranger/ Travelling through this world of woe'. However, beyond this vale of tears, 'there's no sickness, toil or danger/ In that bright land to which I go'. This is a song of hope, but also of resignation: 'I'm only going over Jordan/ I'm only going over home.' The song unfolds in a context where God's promise of heaven and completeness is real: 'I'll soon be free of earthly trials/ My body rest in the old church yard/

---

12 Robyn Marsack (ed.), *Edmund Blunden: Selected Poems* (Manchester: Carcanet, 2018). The poem, written in 1966 and published in 1969, is called 'Ancre Sunshine'.

13 In the film, the song is sung by actor and musical theatre performer Jos Slovick.

I'll drop this cross of self-denial/ And I'll go singing home to God.' However, this soldier is a boy. All of these soldiers, even Schofield, are boys. They should not be singing:

> Well I'm going there
> To meet my Saviour
> Dwell with Him and never roam
> I'm only going over Jordan
> I'm only going over home.

This juxtaposition of youth which embraces the fate of the old is a grotesque juxtaposition, but the song is also the only thing that is apt to the reality. We may feel that we are very far from the vulnerabilities, precarities, griefs and grotesquery of war. However, are we? Really? We who have lived and grown up in privileged countries like the UK have perhaps spent too long imagining that we are not grotesque or that our ways of going on are not precarious. Yet, they hold such things within them. The impact of a virus across the globe in 2020 indicates that. And what is adequate in the end? I think God's promises. I too, like the soldiers in that wood before the surety of their death, want to sing:

> I know dark clouds will gather 'round me
> I know my way is rough and steep
> But golden fields lie just before me
> Where God's redeemed shall ever sleep.

10

The Precariousness of It All
(or, The Odd God of Oxgodby)

This is the chapter I never expected to write. Indeed, this book, as planned, was supposed to be nine chapters long. Circumstances – the most terrifically unanticipated circumstances – require me to revise that plan. I suppose I should have realized that 'book plans', as much as any aspect of life, are as precarious as anything else.

As I write this, I have not been out of doors for nearly a month and I, like everyone, am full of grief and bewilderment and dislocation. I live a kind of persistent, subtle trauma. I live an endless Holy Saturday. A day can feel like a week. A week like a month. There are days when I – normally a driven, energetic and dynamic person – am exhausted by four in the afternoon. I both sleep more and sleep less. I have more time and I have less time. All the things I had in the diary have disappeared and yet I have never been busier. My bed is covered in books I've read a dozen times before, yet when I settle down to read, I can hardly concentrate. I watch ridiculous, escapist box sets that I would never have watched before. I feel close to tears watching absurd home-made lockdown videos on the internet. I want rest. I want exercise. I want to go out. I want to stay in. I want touch. Oh, God, I want touch, and yet I am fearful of it. I want to meet people through other means than via a screen, though sometimes I feel strangely encouraged by seeing another person via Zoom or Facetime or Google Hangout. I feel held in the present. I feel nostalgic. Not least among the things I feel nostalgic for is a sense of a future.

It is too soon for anyone confidently to assess the theological, philosophical or psychological significance of the Covid-19 pandemic of 2020. We are not yet even in a position to assess the economic and public health significance of it. The 'meaning' of the pandemic will almost certainly be the work of years to come. For, as it is placed in its historical and cultural contexts, it may yet be read as a blip or (more likely) as a signal of the conditions under which people shall live in the twenty-first century. Certainly, it is surely the definitive end of what might be called the 'Long Twentieth Century', if that had not already ended.[1] However, even at this early stage in the emergent world one finds oneself in – where no one still quite knows the trajectory of our viral world – it is surely clear that the coronavirus is a fundamental restatement of the world's precarity.

As my opening remarks indicate, there is a sense in which I, and many others, am simply living in shock and grief. What has happened to 'the Church' during this time of virus is, in wider societal terms, hardly a central narrative. However, in some ways the Church's negotiation of conditions of virus offers a striking vignette about the bewildering effects this viral upheaval has generated. Pretty much all churches – Catholic, Liberal, Evangelical, Charismatic, and so on – have traditionally been defined by their capacity to gather together physically. They gather for worship and to be fed. However, within the space of a couple of weeks, the Church found itself moving from holding full services with some distancing and hygiene regulations through to a couple of people in a building attempting to stream a Eucharist or Praise Service, through to solitary clergy broadcasting from hastily arranged domestic oratories. Even if, by the time this book sees publication, these restrictions have been lifted, these shifts reordered the

---

1 My own perception is that, in privileged nations like the UK, the Long Twentieth Century was over by circa 2016. As a sign of this, consider the obsessions among younger generations with the 1980s and 1990s (see shows like *Stranger Things*, and the curious millennial addiction to *Friends*). These decades seem to function for many as the last with open textures of hope and promise, and a sense of potential and future.

embodied facts of the gathered community in ways surely none could quite have imagined. Clever people might talk blithely about the Universal Church or a great Cloud of Witnesses or the power of 'spiritual communion', but for most of the people of God, 'Church' is a proximal matter. We draw close to one another physically. It is haptic too. There is touch and tenderness, and there is feasting, even in Lent. Digital bodies are all very well, spiritual ones too. But dear Lord, is there anything like being fed in the flesh?

So quickly, churches became out of bounds, and one became nostalgic for the days when one was allowed to enter the building simply to pray. Nothing like this had been seen since the thirteenth century. Weddings and baptisms that I was due to preside at were cancelled or postponed. The last funeral I took before I went into total lockdown was meant to be in church with over 120 mourners. The deceased was a beloved church member with friends all over south Manchester. For safety reasons, it became a crem funeral with a single-figure attendance, immediate family only. Understandably and rightly, the Church's leadership have sought to indicate that – in the midst of viral restrictions – we remain the Church, and that we simply have to find new ways of being that which we always were. New ways of being old. There has been, thus far, so much promise in this.

Perhaps one of the things the Church has begun to recover – though how often have we said this? – is a sense of lament. Because, for all our digital wonders and the profound sense in which prayer is the given and the call, many of us feel like exiles from our altars. As the Israelites knew, out of exile may come lament and out of lament a new way of listening to God's word. As Walter Brueggemann said, speaking of the book of Lamentations in which the speaker expresses pain over a bereft Jerusalem:

> Cathartic utterances are ... an honest and courageous practice of prayer. They offer an opportunity for turning brutalised loss into an act of faith that may in turn issue into positive energy. These speech practices give us a way to vent our rage

at loss without letting it escalate into actions that will hurt our neighbours.[2]

Perhaps out of lament a new song for the Church may yet come, more attentive to the call of Christ.

It is worth also acknowledging that I have prayed more and more fervently during this time of lockdown than I have in years. Also, in the past few weeks, I have been an old-school pastor, connected with my cure of souls, more than at any time in the previous decade. I have picked up the phone and listened and engaged in a way I never had time to do before. There is a sense in which being more like an anchorite than a post-modern über-busy priest has taught me what really matters. However, as I write this I am also exhausted by this change. It can be exhilarating to live in strange times. One can become an adrenaline junkie. However, strange and traumatic times also call for crisis mode; for survival. I feel like I'm newly ordained again, learning to live ministry all over again. And I feel grief and trauma and loss and bewilderment too. I'm holding things together for the sake of my little flock and because I think God calls me to do so. However, I know also there will be a price. And the price will be paid in the body, mine and others. God's too. That cost is coming.

I acknowledge that this is a vignette which explores what it feels like to live upheaval in a very privileged context. I, like most priests, am profoundly privileged. I have not lost my 'livelihood'. Though I am housebound, I am housebound in a large and rather lovely house. I have the wonderful challenge of working with colleagues, lay and ordained, in creative and rich ways of serving God in a time of crisis. Some of the things my colleagues and I have learned in the midst of crisis will be very significant for ministry in years to come. Many other people are less privileged. While I have, as a result of disability and major surgeries, experienced times when I've been

---

2 Quoted in *Celtic Daily Prayer Book Two*, the resource of the Northumbria Community. Originally published as 'Conversations among Exiles', *The Christian Century*, 2–9 July 1997.

housebound, I do not live that as a matter of course. Many do. I have the good fortune of being an introvert too. I'm happy with my own company most of the time, and there is a kind of privilege in living alone at this time. I know that those trying to hold down a job while trying to home-school children face much greater challenges. It is also a signal of privilege that 'self-isolation' and 'self-distancing' is possible at all. In many nations, especially in the global South, this is just not going to be possible because of the realities of how homes and work operate. Potentially, millions will die.

The trauma is real, though, and life in a time of Covid-19 is a time of grief. Part of the signal of that is the profound unsettlement encountered in the body. It is a trauma in individual bodies, corporate bodies, as well as in the body politic. I'm not sure anyone, least of all the leaders of the nation themselves, could have imagined the most libertarian government in Conservative history acting as agents and promoters of community welfare, however hedged around that has been. This disruption in the economic and political body has been so huge that it is tempting to speculate what the social side-effects will be. Might we become more serious about community again? Might we all become more 'small "c" conservative'? Might we come so to cherish the return of birds and peace and quiet to our gardens and streets that we shall relate to the natural world afresh? Or, once this is over, might we go on a wild spree utterly careless to the effects on the planet? Will we be able to talk of 'we' and 'us' at all? Might we – given the experiences of the post-Great War and Second War generations – become raging hedonists or artists with a new flowering of freedom? Might our war metaphors fail? That is not for now, as far as I'm concerned. I'm more interested, right now, in what it might mean to live well in the shadow of what the virus has exposed: the unavoidability of precariousness and grief.

I read somewhere that if a virus were the size of a five-pence piece, a bacterium would be the size of a dinner plate, and the average human would be 200 kilometres tall. There is something utterly stunning about the fact that something so tiny, and seemingly insignificant, could cause stock markets to groan, the price of oil to tumble and force governments to persuade, cajole and, in some cases, enforce their publics to stay indoors and away from other people in a kind of house arrest. A tiny organism has subverted our species' seemingly deepest instinct for physical contact and made one of our defining features – our capacity to derive pleasure, encouragement and cheer from contact, congregation and touch – a genuine danger. It is as if it has taken one of the tiniest creatures on the planet to demonstrate that our strategies of power, control, safety and surety are contingent. Prior to the coronavirus pandemic I suspect many would have blithely consigned the idea of 'pandemic' or 'plague' to history, something applicable to 1918 or 1665 or 1347. Such a perspective has been definitively called out. We do not live outside history. There is no 'out' from the precarious. Precarity is part of the quiddity of creation.

I know I must be careful in what I say here. I know Covid-19 presents the latest iteration of threats to human health and that those who will face its effects disproportionately will be those with little economic power or access to medicine. I do not want in any way to laud 'Covid-19', as if it gives privileged people like me an opportunity to grandstand and say, 'I told you so. I told you it was all precarious.' That would be tasteless at the best of times. Given that our friends and neighbours – both locally and globally – are dying or are finding themselves falling into anxiety and mental distress because of the effects of isolation and limit, it would be deeply offensive. Given that some people with enormous wealth and access to superb medical care will escape the worst effects, smug claims about what the virus teaches human beings about the precarious would be monstrous.

I simply want to acknowledge the precarious as a fact of bodies and a world of limit and that – if the body and the world is to be good and holy at all – living well requires relationship, community and intimacy. For all the wonders of technology – and how I, as a non-digital native, have given thanks for their existence at this time! – I cannot accept that it is enough. Life in a time of virus and self-isolation and social distancing reveals the wonderful precariousness of bodies, and part of that precariousness is the extent to which we so readily become dazzled by the blur between the real and the hyper-real, the unreal and the surreal. It is through the line of our fragile bodies – that mortality, that materiality, that capacity for our bodies to be overwhelmed by disease – that promise and hope is to be found. Grief – social, personal, cultural – is a mark of our capacity for holiness. Grief is a mark of our capacity to grow into the likeness of Christ.

I've spent a lot of time recently considering the power of the proximal and the haptic. The proximal can be understood, in anatomical terms, as referring to that which draws closest to the centre of the body. It also has implications of attachment: the proximal is that which is nearest or near to the point of attachment. It can have temporal implications: of something that is 'nigh'. I know that in spiritual direction circles, especially those influenced by St Ignatius, the notion of 'attachments' is carefully interrogated. They are not merely neutral matters. We can have attachments that get in the way of our relationship with God and those attachments – to possessions, to intense relationship – can be genuinely multiform. However, I sense that not least among the things that this time of virus and isolation has revealed is the holiness of some kinds of attachment. Indeed, I want to cry out for the holiness of bodies. I long for the proximal. And, yes, the proximal can be revealed through screens, but can there be anything quite like the proximal known through touch and taste and smell? Oh, to have God on my tongue; oh, to place my hands in his side; oh, to anoint his body with perfume.

The haptic, of course, relates to our sense of touch, derived from *haptikos*, 'able to come into contact with'. That itself has an etymological history in *haptein*, to fasten. Touch always has dangerous, precarious and risky connotations. Unwanted touch can be utterly vile and entail violation. Sticky hands are rarely attractive hands. If we all have unclean hands, how quickly they become grubby. Yet, part of the potency of touch lies in its precarity. For it is also the place we can negotiate that which helps us 'hold fast' to the holy and allows God to 'hold fast' to us. As I write this, I haven't physically touched another human being for weeks. I know that it may yet be many months before I touch another human's hand, hug someone, receive a kiss. Before they hold me. I know, also, that there are many ways of being 'touched' and touching others. But I feel starved too. I am so hungry. I may have permission to preside at Mass 'solo', as it were, on behalf of the cure of souls, but I am so hungry for more. I am hungry for the feast of Eucharist and for Peace and to be proximal to the fullness of God's touch shown in the Body of Christ. Oh, for the table around which we gather and share a cup and broken bread, passed hand to hand. To repeat: digital bodies are all very wonderful, spiritual ones too. But, dear Lord, is there anything like being fed in the flesh?

I have struggled to read during this time of isolation. There is a particular kind of relationship with paper and word I've struggled to sustain. I think my eyes are so tired after concentrating on faces shown on screen in Zoom or Teams meetings that I cannot be present to the word. I've generally gone back to comfort reading. The academic Alison Light calls Golden Age detective fiction the 'literature of convalescence', and in this time of healing and loss, I've found those classic mysteries written by Agatha Christie and such like very comforting. One other book has come back to me again: J. L. Carr's *A Month in the Country*.[3] It is one of my favourite books and I wrote about it in *Fierce Imaginings*, in the context of post-traumatic stress disorder, 'shell shock' and healing.[4]

A Month in the Country is, if you don't know, set in North Yorkshire in the summer of 1920. It revolves around the friendship between two men, Birkin and Moon. Both are traumatized Great War veterans and each has come to the village of Oxgodby for work: Birkin to uncover a 500-year-old wall painting on the village church and Moon to find the lost medieval grave of a notable local resident. Both the novel and

---

3 J. L. Carr, *A Month in the Country* (Harmondsworth: Penguin, 1980).

4 See Rachel Mann, *Fierce Imaginings* (London: Darton, Longman & Todd, 2017), pp. 114–16.

the beautiful 1987 film adaptation, starring Colin Firth and Kenneth Branagh, are at their strongest when presenting the simple dissonance between the men's recent past and people's desire to get on with their lives, amid the beauty of the English countryside. It has always struck me as an intimate study into what the healing of traumatized bodies looks like in a war-blasted, precarious world. In *Fierce Imaginings* I wrote:

> Over the summer the two men begin to heal, not least through a process of 'substitution' – they find in their respective work a place to negotiate their pain. They expose their trauma by allowing their work to speak 'into' them and their trauma into their work. For Birkin [an atheist] it is in the slow work of revealing a Medieval 'Judgment' Wall in the Church. He slowly exposes an artist's rendering of a world-view long since lost, both figuratively and literally, to the modern world.[5]

What has stunned me on re-reading it in a time of coronavirus is how impossible it has been to get through many pages without weeping. I've always found this book funny and gentle and beautiful, and I've always shed a tear at the end. However, I've never before felt broken on almost every simple, subtle page. It's taken me a while to figure out why Carr's book has affected me so deeply. It is because it is a study in the power of the proximal and the haptic. It is a book about relationships between humans – most of them damaged in some way – but also about the relationships a person can have with buildings and material and visual culture. The central character, Birkin, who initially has a war-generated stutter, finds healing in part through his relationship with the 'Doom Wall' he uncovers. He begins to find healing as his craftsman's knife exposes and comes into relationship with a world older and deeper than the traumatized reality he has so recently lived through. He places his shattered narrative in another story, one that is uncompromising and ancient.

---

5 Mann, *Fierce Imaginings*, p. 115.

For the field archaeologist Moon, a war hero who was sent to prison in the final stages of the war for homosexuality, a kind of healing comes not so much in finding the lost grave he seeks, but in finding that its contents are subversive and unexpected. Moon, a man who sleeps in a surrogate grave and who has seen too much death, meets death again in the form of a medieval skeleton. The encounter offers an unexpected revelation: that the body was buried outside holy ground because its owner was a Muslim. On his grave is inscribed, 'I, of all men, the most wretched'. This ancestor of the local landed gentry was no figure of respectability but utterly cast out as other. Moon meets his (and his generation's) historical analogue and is no longer quite so afraid of living.

In a time with limited proximity and a lack of touch, such as the one I currently know, perhaps it is unsurprising that I'm moved by representations of traumatized humans finding healing through relationship, touch and friendship. Birkin and Moon are a study in hauntology: they are haunted by loss and trauma and extreme experience. Even by the end of the novel, both know that neither will ever quite achieve escape velocity from their trauma. Not for a moment do I think my experience is comparable to shell-shocked soldiers, but I am alert to the way in which the Covid-19 crisis has generated feelings of loss and closed-down-ness and a longing for healing. Moon has not achieved escape velocity from the trenches; so much so he still sleeps in a grave-like ditch. There are times when I think I will never – in my own way – relate to the outdoors again; that Covid-19 will for ever make outside and other people feel 'unsafe'.

However, what has most specifically made me cry about *A Month in the Country* is its tender handling of precariousness and of the promise and gift to be found in it when precarity is placed in proper perspective. Birkin is tasked with revealing a medieval work of art that was whitewashed over centuries before. One false touch or slip of his tools and a fragile master-piece will be destroyed. Birkin brings his skill and love and tenderness to bear on something that, for centuries, has been unwanted or seen as embarrassing. Birkin gives himself over to a simple work of uncovering; he places himself in the service of an artist greater than himself. He – an atheist – thereby comes into relationship with an account of holiness and the Divine that has almost been lost. In it he finds the seeds of healing.

Slowly he is brought into a new relationship with the open goodness of precarious life. His hands and tools touch the ancient walls and remove the accretions of centuries to reveal a deeper story. The power of touch is unveiled: the skill of Birkin's hands on the wall, his gift for revealing what is there, as well as the power of an anonymous artist's masterwork, who in return 'touches' the wounded soldier. Carr reveals how touch is a metaphor for the body and for the soul: when we are touched by something we are moved. And the way in which Birkin is moved is by discovering that the world is not closed up and his life is not over. He shall not be utterly defined by trauma. The future remains possible.

There are days when I wonder if I (if any of us) shall ever properly find my (our) way back to the outdoors and to the open riches of the precarity of being a human. *A Month in the Country* models, most of all, how if deep trauma cannot be made commensurate with 'ordinary' life, it can be reckoned with – in some measure – through relationship. As the novel unfolds, and the world turns, memory and past – for ever sullied by violence – slowly reform as less terrifying. At one point, Moon says, 'I tell myself it'll get better as time passes and it sinks further back. But it's got nowhere to sink to, has it?' What Moon and Birkin (and the men and women they represent) discover is that if they can find nowhere in their own traumatized minds for the War to sink, it finds a level in the ancient rhythms and unexpected aporia of landscape and narrative.

I believe that there will be a new day. How could I not and remain a believer? That new day will entail, in part, recovering what is old, very old indeed. That old thing is also the newest thing there is: the Body of Christ, ever ancient, ever new. It is the place where Love's mysteries are found, cherished, negotiated and transformed. The gift of being part of the Body of Christ is that one can embrace one's limit and precariousness.

There is rest there for weary, shattered bodies. One's fragility is held in something greater. As one such shattered body, I cannot say how much I long to see, touch and taste my Lord. I am minded of that old story, told in Eamon Duffy's *The Stripping of the Altars*, about medieval peasants drilling 'squints' in the chancel walls so that they could see the priest consecrate the bread and wine.[6] One is recorded as shouting, as the priest elevated the bread, 'I have seen my Lord!' This time of physical separation has reminded me that I am no more or less sophisticated than that medieval peasant. I too long for encounter. I want taste and touch and all the blessed, fragile wonders our God provides for us. Yes, there will be a new day, and it will be a reckoning with the fragile goodness of God.

However, there will also be echoes of trauma, and echoes of echoes of that trauma. There will simply be trauma. I cannot believe that there won't be a reckoning in the body – the Body of Christ, as well as our particular, individual bodies. That's what trauma does. It works itself out through bones and sinew and flesh. It makes us shake and stumble. We who have known this time of virus and lockdown and physical deprivation may not end up looking exactly like Birkin or Moon or the countless traumatized bodies that crisis and restriction have generated, but I sense many of us will bear a family resemblance. Already, I feel the groans and aches in my own body. Holding the body together – both one's own and those one is called to have responsibility for – is costly. Already, I feel that cost of being on transmit, of loving without taking sufficient care for oneself, and having to learn and relearn new ways of going on. I feel the cost of novelty.

None of us know quite how this is all going to shake down and fall out. I sense that, in my own case, there will be – after the initial crisis is over – a profound need for rest and refreshment. A time of re-scoping will be required. And a time of partying too. I guess what I'm saying is that, if that partying and resting will have a secular holiness – the party on the

---

6 Eamon Duffy, *The Stripping of the Altars*, 2nd edn (London and New Haven, KT: Yale University Press, 2005 (1992)), chapter 1.

street, the reckless abandon of simply going on holiday, the sitting and staring at the sea – there will needs be another kind of feasting. There will be need for communion and the community of God, gathered around the table of our Lord. There will be need for divine food and feasting. It is these things that I sense the true emergence of our futures.

At the outset of this chapter I said that one of the things many of us are nostalgic for is a sense of the future. Well, as with previous catastrophes, the corona pandemic has revealed the limits of meliorist positivism. The world doesn't simply get better and better. I suspect most of us didn't buy into such crap anyway. The world – in the face of climate change and groaning economic systems – already feels too precarious. The technocrat's or the economist's vision of a world shaped around 'better' or 'growth without end' fails to convince. When people like me say, 'God, yesterday, tomorrow, today', we speak of and into a different economy and a richer picture of the future of grace. This is a world that tumbles and creaks and groans with its fragility yet is sustained and shot through with God. This is a world where bread for today and for tomorrow is enough, more than enough. This is a world where the body – ever precarious, ever living, ever wondrous – is enough, more than enough. This is God, who, as the Book of Common Prayer has it, is World Without End.

Postscript

I am sitting in my stall at our regular midweek Eucharist. There are half a dozen people in the congregation; people who have been connected with the church where I serve for much of their lives. They are faithful and committed and each one of them is quite lovely. They are themselves in their quirkiness and I have come to love them all. However, I am a little distracted. Just the week before I had a bit of a health scare – some potential issues with my heart and blood – which, though I'm glad to say came to nothing, has given me pause for thought as I enter my fifth decade. I am not quite present in my usual way.

As I sit in my stall, my colleague, our new curate, shares some reflections on that day's Gospel according to Mark. Distracted though I am, as he speaks I begin to come into focus and attention. His comments centre on the dynamic between how we might be caught up in the demands of the world – all its busyness, business and need – and the call to retreat and pray and listen. It is a fine reflection worthy, I reflect, of a grand setting, a cathedral say; worthy of a large congregation; worthy of a High Mass with smells and bells; and he offers it to us, half a dozen at a midweek service in a small parish in south Manchester.

And, as I listen, and then we move through the Creed and into the prayers and finally the Eucharist itself, I find I am moved. I am drawn deeper and deeper into something. I am entranced, almost enraptured, if that doesn't sound completely ridiculous. In the midst of the ordinariness, the week-by-week conventionality of this service (perhaps, because of it) – with all the coughs and splutters one expects among people gathered in a cold church on a Wednesday in January, with the shuffles and the old ladies talking to each other as my colleague and I set up the altar – I am entranced by the abundance of it all. By how this *is* God's abundance. This *is* community. This *is* participation and the fullness of life.

I suspect that were a stranger to walk in on this service, whether they be a person of faith or not, that they would not be struck immediately by abundance. Certainly, they might be rather taken aback, even stunned, by the glories of the building – the way its modernist vision meets medieval ideas of space and wonder, the way the colours seem to model both order and riot – but what, at a human level, might they see? A small group of humans, mostly in their seventies and above, and a couple of clergy quietly going about the work of a priest.

I suspect they would not be overwhelmed by any obvious sense that this is a thriving parish; they would see a kind of microcosm of the twenty-first-century Church: a handful of old people in woolly hats, struggling along with the aid of wheeled walkers, ministered to by a middle-aged, rather clapped-out cleric and a young, hopeful newbie. They would not see glory, but retreat. They would see church on the High Dependency Unit or – to mix metaphors – a glorious building-turned-care-home. They would not see the hub of any great movement or a shiny place. There are no lanyards here or scintillating, even white smiles. There is quiet and a bit of a draught.

But, as the service unfolds, I remain breathless with abundance. Perhaps it is a symptom of my final delusion, a decay in my perceptions so advanced that I treat desperation as glory, failure as hope. Have I become like those clerical figures in the underworld in Pullman's *His Dark Materials* books who claim that perdition actually is glory? These are the dead held in the underworld who insist that this *is* heaven if only those trapped there could let the scales fall from their eyes. Or, if not quite that, that such purgatory is a necessary step towards transformation.

However, I don't think I am trapped in those sorts of delusion. I know what this service is. I know that we are ordinary human beings enacting a 2,000-year-old liturgical act in a small parish. We do not have the resources available to ancient foundations. Despite the gifts of my talented colleague and the experience I bring to bear on the proceedings, I know that we do not achieve anything exquisite in our celebration of the Holy Mysteries. This remains the location of Love's Mysteries. But still I cannot escape an encounter with abundance. And it takes my breath away. I feel like I am being given everything I shall ever need and more.

I wrote that reflection back in the middle of February 2020, before everything changed and we locked up our church for a season. When I wrote it, 'Covid-19' and 'coronavirus' seemed very far away still. As I write this updated postscript, in some ways that meditation seems to belong to another time. I still stand by it, though. If the coronavirus pandemic represents a particularly pressing encounter with generalized and particular grief and precariousness, I remain convinced it is not *sui generis*. It is the latest moment in the ongoing grief and fragility of the human story. And I remain convinced that it is possible for us to encounter abundance in the midst of our countless griefs.

To return back to where this book began: grief at its broadest is about bodies encountering the facts of loss, limit and fragility. It is a theme of the world. When one is born, one loses the womb. One is born into grief. That first cry we all make as a baby is a cry of grief as much as a cry of hope. I'm not sure we ever recover from this first encounter with loss. Nor should we. Otherwise, we never quite learn how to live. And, call me a fool, a bloody old fool if you will, but in the midst of all the mess and misery, sorrow, loss and this world of grief, there is another song. That song sings of the abundance of love.

This is a song that holds all the stories we shall ever own and those that we, through shame or failure, cannot; this is the song that sings all the griefs I and all of us shall ever know; this is the song that does not need to be sung for it is always being sung in the silence of the universe, in the stirrings of birds, and the breeze and storm which tickle and shake trees; it is the song of industry and of rest. It is the sustaining song of the world. It is the world. It is the world God made and which she beheld as good. It is the universe hallowed and shot through with glory and grace and wounds. It is Christ who holds the world's griefs in his wounds, and continues to cry out for a world of wounds at the Father's throne. It is the little story and the great one. It is a line of poetry and an epic. It is a word barely mumbled and the grandest novel. It is silence and the most riven cry. It is the Word that dwells and drifts and anchors. It is the song which sings us in all our moments – our births, our deaths, our dreams, our triumphs and failures; in our competence and our ineptitude. It is the bread and cup that sustains us and exposes our limitations. It is the precarious body that cannot be destroyed.

Anthony Powell closes his *A Dance to the Music of Time* sequence with a quote from Robert Burton's extraordinary seventeenth-century text, *The Anatomy of Melancholy*, a polymathic, sprawling work that analyses what might now be called clinical depression. The central character of the *Dance*, Nick Jenkins, who has travelled from youth to old age through Powell's pages, calls the passage I shall share 'torrential'. Burton's words are a reminder that in all times, all things are going on, and much that changes never changes in great substance:

I hear new news every day, and those ordinary rumours of war, plagues, fires, inundations, thefts, murders, massacres, meteors, comets, spectrums, prodigies, apparitions, of towns taken, cities besieged in France, Germany, Turkey, Persia, Poland, &c., daily musters and preparations, and such like, which these tempestuous times afford, battles fought, so many men slain, monomachies, shipwrecks, piracies, and sea-fights, peace, leagues, stratagems, and fresh alarms. A vast confusion of vows, wishes, actions, edicts, petitions, lawsuits, pleas, laws, proclamations, complaints, grievances, are daily brought to our ears. New books every day, pamphlets, currantoes, stories, whole catalogues of volumes of all sorts, new paradoxes, opinions, schisms, heresies, controversies in philosophy, religion, &c. Now come tidings of weddings, maskings, mummeries, entertainments, jubilees, embassies, tilts and tournaments, trophies, triumphs, revels, sports, plays: then again, as in a new shifted scene, treasons, cheating tricks, robberies, enormous villanies in all kinds, funerals, burials, deaths of Princes, new discoveries, expeditions; now comical then tragical matters. To-day we hear of new Lords and officers created, to-morrow of some great men deposed, and then again of fresh honours conferred; one is let loose, another imprisoned; one purchaseth, another breaketh: he thrives, his neighbour turns bankrupt; now plenty, then again dearth and famine; one runs, another rides, wrangles, laughs, weeps &c.

Burton is right, of course. Precariousness and grief and fragility and lability are the markers of human culture and society. We flip and we flop. We fight and we make temporary truces. But I also want to say that those of us who hold fast to a God of grace and love – a God whose promise flows through our griefs and fractures – are no less right. God is fact and promise. And God, despite our best efforts, cannot be redacted out of the story or simply got rid of as an embarrassment to one and all. I know many have tried, both those who are religious and those who are not. I know why we do it: because we cannot bear what Love, in its fullness, is like. So, we ... you ... I ... break his ... her ... their ... fragile body. But she will not stay still or stay down. She rises again and, to our alarm and sometimes to our delight, greets us as friends and lovers in the Garden of Good News and Resurrection. And we dare not remain the same.

Select Bibliography

Stephen T. Asma, *On Monsters: An Unnatural History of Our Worst Fears* (Oxford and New York: Oxford University Press, 2009).

Roland Barthes, *Camera Lucida*, trans. Richard Howard (London: Vintage Classics, 2020 (1982)).

Lyn M. Bechtel, 'Rethinking the Interpretation of Genesis 2.4B—3.24', in Athalya Brenner (ed.), *A Feminist Companion to Genesis* (Sheffield: Sheffield Academic Press, 1997 (1993)), pp. 77–118.

Lauren Berlant, *Cruel Optimism* (Durham, NC: Duke University Press, 2011).

Adele Berlin and Marc Zvi Brettler (eds), *The Jewish Study Bible*, 2nd edn (Oxford: Oxford University Press, 2014).

Athalya Brenner (ed.), *A Feminist Companion to Genesis* (Sheffield: Sheffield Academic Press, 1997 (1993)).

Elisabeth Bronfen, *Over Her Dead Body: Death, Femininity, and the Aesthetic* (Manchester: Manchester University Press, 1992).

Judith Butler, *Frames of War: When is Life Grievable?* (London and New York: Verso, 2010).

——, *Notes Towards a Performative Theory of Assembly* (Cambridge, MA: Harvard University Press, 2015).

——, *Precarious Life: The Powers of Mourning and Violence* (London and New York: Verso, 2006 (2004)).

J. L. Carr, *A Month in the Country* (Harmondsworth: Penguin, 1980).

Colleen M. Conway, 'The Construction of Gender in the New Testament', in Adrian Thatcher (ed.), *The Oxford Handbook of Theology, Sexuality and Gender* (Oxford: Oxford University Press, 2015), pp. 222–38.

Eamon Duffy, *The Stripping of the Altars*, 2nd edn (London and New Haven, CT: Yale University Press, 2005 (1992)).

Mark Fisher, *The Weird and the Eerie* (London: Repeater Books, 2016).

Paul Fussell, *Wartime* (Oxford: Oxford University Press, 1989).

Wil Gafney, *Womanist Midrash: A Reintroduction to the Women of the Torah and the Throne* (Louisville, KY: Westminster John Knox Press, 2017).

Luce Irigaray, *The Forgetting of Air in Martin Heidegger*, trans. Mary Beth Mader (London: The Athlone Press, 1999 (1983)).

Christina Lamb, *Our Bodies, Their Battlefield* (London: William Collins, 2020).

Bruno Latour, *Pandora's Hope: Essays on the Reality of Science Studies* (London and Cambridge, MA: Harvard University Press, 1999).

Deborah Lupton, *Medicine as Culture: Illness, Disease and the Body*, 3rd edn (New York: Sage Publications, 2012).

Rachel Mann, *Dazzling Darkness* (Glasgow: Wild Goose, 2012).

————, *Fierce Imaginings* (London: Darton, Longman and Todd, 2017).

————, *A Kingdom of Love* (Manchester: Carcanet, 2019).

————, 'The Priest Attends to the Word: Parish Poetics', in Jessica Martin and Sarah Coakley (eds), *For God's Sake: Re-Imagining Priesthood and Prayer in a Changing Church* (Norwich: Canterbury Press, 2016), pp. 78–91.

Avishai Margalit, *The Ethics of Memory* (Cambridge, MA: Harvard University Press, 2002).

Ruth Mazo Karras, 'Reproducing Medieval Christianity', in Adrian Thatcher (ed.), *The Oxford Handbook of Theology, Sexuality and Gender* (Oxford: Oxford University Press, 2015), pp. 271–86.

Roberta McGrath, *Seeing Her Sex: Medical Archives and the Female Body* (Manchester and New York: Manchester University Press, 2002).

Janet Morley, *All Desires Known* (London: SPCK, 1988).

Karen O'Donnell, *Broken Bodies: The Eucharist, Mary and the Body in Trauma Theology* (London: SCM Press, 2019).

Patrick Parrinder, *James Joyce* (Cambridge: Cambridge University Press, 2008).

Yopie Prins and Maeera Shreiber, *Dwelling in Possibility: Women Poets and Critics on Poetry*, Reading Women Writing (London and Ithaca, NY: Cornell University Press, 1997).

Shelly Rambo, *Spirit and Trauma: A Theology of Remaining* (Louisville, KY: Westminster John Knox Press, 2010).

————, *Resurrecting Trauma: Living in the Afterlife of Trauma* (Waco, TX: Baylor University Press, 2017).

Gillian Rose, *The Broken Middle: Out of Our Ancient Society* (Oxford: Wiley-Blackwell, 1992).

————, *Mourning Becomes the Law: Philosophy and Representation* (Cambridge: Cambridge University Press, 1996).

Kate Schick, *Gillian Rose: A Good Enough Justice* (Edinburgh: Edinburgh University Press, 2012).

Frances Shaw, *Wearing Well: Exploring the Biblical Imagery of Clothing* (Vancouver: Regent College Publishing, 2019).

Phillis Sheppard in Pamela Lightsey, *Our Lives Matter: A Womanist Queer Theology* (Eugene, OR: Pickwick, 2015).

Margrit Shildrick, *Embodying the Monster: Encounters with the Vulnerable Self* (London: Sage Publications, 2002).

———, *Leaky Bodies and Boundaries: Feminism, Postmodernism and (Bio)Ethics* (London: Routledge, 1997).

Adrian Thatcher, *Redeeming Gender* (Oxford: Oxford University Press, 2016).

Phyllis Trible, *God and the Rhetoric of Sexuality* (Philadelphia, PA: Fortress Press, 1978).

W. H. Vanstone, *Love's Endeavour, Love's Expense* (London: Darton, Longman & Todd, 2007 (1977)).

Ludwig Wittgenstein, *Philosophical Investigations* (Cambridge: Cambridge University Press, 1953).